FOURTH GENERAL CONFERENCE OF LATIN AMERICAN BISHOPS

Santo Domingo, Dominican Republic
October 12-28, 1992

NEW EVANGELIZATION
HUMAN DEVELOPMENT
CHRISTIAN CULTURE

D1226041

Secretariat
Bishops' Committee for the Church in Latin America
National Conference of Catholic Bishops

The NCCB Secretariat of the Committee for the Church in Latin America, in fulfilling its mandate to disseminate information concerning the Church in Latin America, has authorized the publication of an English translation of the documents arising from the Fourth General Conference of Latin American Episcopates held in Santo Domingo, Dominican Republic, October 12-28, 1992. This present text of the *Santo Domingo Conclusions* has been reviewed and approved by Mr. Thomas Quigley, of the Office for International Justice and Peace, the United States Catholic Conference, and is authorized for publication by the undersigned.

Monsignor Robert N. Lynch
General Secretary
NCCB/USCC

July 9, 1993

Translation of the Spanish text *Santo Domingo Conclusiones* by Phillip Berryman.

ISBN 1-55586-593-3

CONTENTS

LETTER OF POPE JOHN PAUL II TO THE BISHOPS OF LATIN AMERICA

To the Diocesan Bishops of Latin America

On the occasion of the Fifth Centenary of the Evangelization of America, I convoked the Fourth General Conference of the Latin American Episcopate, whose goal was to study, in the light of Christ, "the same yesterday, today, and forever" (Heb 13:8), the great themes of the new evangelization, human development, and Christian culture.

Divine Providence gave me the consolation of being able personally to inaugurate this assembly in Santo Domingo on 12 October. On the 28th of that same month the Conference's work was finished, and the presidents sent me the conclusions that the bishops present had drafted.

I was greatly pleased to see the profound pastoral concern with which my brothers in the Episcopate examined the topics that I had proposed, in order to contribute to the development of the life of the Church in Latin America in view of the present and the future.

The final texts of this Conference, whose publication I have authorized, can now give direction to the pastoral work of each diocesan bishop in Latin America. Each diocesan pastor, together with his priests, "his co-workers" (cf. *Lumen Gentium*, 28), and the other members of the particular Church that has been entrusted to him, will make the discernment necessary to see what is most useful and urgent in the particular situation of his diocese.

A broad consensus among the bishops of the particular Churches in a given country could also lead to joint pastoral formulas or plans, always with respect for the identity of each diocese and the pastoral authority of the bishop, who is the visible center of unity and, at the same time, its hierarchical bond with the Successor of Peter and the universal Church (cf. *Lumen Gentium*, 23).

As is obvious, the Conclusions of the Santo Domingo Conference must be analyzed in the light of the magisterium of the universal Church and should be implemented in fidelity to existing canonical discipline.

For my part, I trust that the pastoral solicitude of the bishops of Latin America will give all the particular Churches of the continent a renewed commitment to the new evangelization, human development, and the Christian culture.

May Jesus Christ, our Lord, Evangelizer and Savior, be at the center of the Church's life today, as yesterday and forever.

May the Virgin most holy, who was always at the side of her divine Son, accompany the pastors and faithful in their pilgrimage toward the Lord.

From the Vatican, 10 November 1992, memorial of St. Leo the Great, Pope and Doctor of the Church

IOANNES PAULUS II

OPENING ADDRESS OF
THE HOLY FATHER

1. Under the guidance of the Spirit, to whom we have fervently appealed to enlighten the work of this important ecclesial assembly, we are inaugurating the Fourth General Conference of the Latin American Episcopate. In doing so, we turn our eyes and our hearts to Jesus Christ, "the same yesterday, today, and forever" (Heb 13:8). He is the beginning and end, the Alpha and Omega (cf. Rv 21:6), the fullness of evangelization, "the very first and the greatest evangelizer; he was so through and through: to perfection and to the point of the sacrifice of his earthly life" (*Evangelii Nuntiandi,* 7).

In this ecclesial gathering, we have a very vivid sense of the presence of Jesus Christ, Lord of history. In his name, the bishops of Latin America met at their previous assemblies: Rio de Janeiro (1955); Medellín (1968); and Puebla (1979). In his name, we are now meeting in Santo Domingo to deal with the issues of "New Evangelization, Human Development, Christian Culture," which encompass the major challenges that the Church will be confronting due to the new situations emerging in Latin America and around the world.

This is a time of grace, my dear brothers, for all of us and for the Church in the Americas. Indeed, it is a time of grace for the universal Church, which is accompanying us with its prayer and with that deep communion of hearts that the Holy Spirit engenders in all the members of the one body of Christ. It is a time of grace and of great responsibility. The third millennium is now within sight. If divine providence has called us together so that we may give thanks to God for the five hundred years of faith and Christian life on the American continent, it is perhaps even more true to say that we have been called together for interior renewal, to "judge the signs of the times" (Mt 16:3). Indeed, the call to the new evangelization is first and foremost a call to conversion. For through the witness of a Church that is ever more faithful to its own identity and that manifests itself with ever greater vitality, the individuals and peoples of Latin America and of the whole world will be able to continue finding Jesus Christ, and in him the truth of their calling and their hope, and the way to a nobler humanity.

Looking toward Christ, keeping "our eyes fixed on Jesus, the leader and perfecter of faith" (Heb 12:2), we follow the path traced by the Second Vatican Council. The thirtieth anniversary of its solemn inauguration was yesterday. Hence, in inaugurating this splendid assembly, I want to recall those heartfelt words pronounced by my venerable predecessor Pope Paul VI at the opening of the second session of the council:

Christ!
Christ, our beginning.
Christ, our life and our guide.
Christ, our hope and our end. . . .
May no other light hover over this assembly
than that of Christ, light of the world.
May no other truth draw our minds,
than the words of the Lord, our one Master.
May no other hope sustain us,
than that which bolsters our weakness through his word.

I. JESUS CHRIST, YESTERDAY, TODAY, AND FOREVER

2. This conference is meeting to celebrate Jesus Christ, to thank God for his presence in these lands of the Americas, where the message of salvation began to spread five hundred years ago. It is meeting to celebrate the planting of the Church, which has furnished the New World with such abundant fruits of holiness and love during these five centuries.

Jesus Christ is the eternal truth who became manifest in the fullness of time. It was specifically to transmit the good news to all peoples that he founded his Church with the specific mission to evangelize: "Go into the whole world and proclaim the Gospel to every creature" (Mk 16:15). These words can be said to contain the solemn proclamation of evangelization. Thus, the Church began the great task of evangelization on the day when the apostles received the Holy Spirit. St. Paul expresses it in a crisp, emblematic expression: *"Evangelizare Iesum Christum,"* "to proclaim Jesus Christ" (Gal 1:16). This is what the disciples of the Lord have done in all ages and throughout the world.

3. The year 1492 marks a key date in this unique process. On October 12— exactly five centuries ago today—Admiral Christopher Columbus, with the three caravels from Spain, arrived at these lands and planted the cross of Christ. Nevertheless, strictly speaking, evangelization began with the second journey of the explorers, who were accompanied by the first missionaries. Thus, began the sowing of the precious gift of faith. How can we fail to thank God for that, along with you, my dear brother bishops, you who today embody in Santo Domingo all the particular churches of Latin America! How can we

fail to give thanks for the abundant fruits of the seed sown over the course of these five centuries by so many dauntless missionaries!

With the coming of the gospel to the Americas, the history of salvation expands, the family of God grows and multiplies "so that the grace bestowed in abundance on more and more people may cause the thanksgiving to overflow for the glory of God" (2 Cor 4:15). The peoples of the New World were "new peoples . . . entirely unknown to the Old World until 1492," but they were "known to God from all eternity, and he had embraced them with the Fatherhood that the Son had revealed in the fullness of time (cf. Gal 4:4)" (*Homily,* January 1, 1992). In the peoples of the Americas, God has chosen for himself a new people whom he has brought into his redemptive plan and made sharers in his Spirit. Through evangelization and faith in Christ, God has renewed his covenant with Latin America.

Thus, we thank God for the throng of evangelizers who had to leave their homeland and who gave their life in order to sow the new life of faith, hope, and love in the New World. They were not drawn by the legend of El Dorado or personal interests, but by the pressing call to evangelize some brothers and sisters who did not yet know Jesus Christ. They proclaimed "the kindness and generous love of God our savior" (Ti 3:4) to peoples, some of whom even offered human sacrifices to their gods. With their lives and their word, they gave witness to that humanity that results from encounter with Christ. By their witness and their preaching, the number of men and women who were opened to the grace of Christ multiplied like "the stars in the sky and as countless as the sands on the seashore" (Heb 11:12).

4. Since the first steps of evangelization, the Catholic Church, prompted by fidelity to the Spirit of Christ, has been a tireless defender of the Indians, a protector of the values present in their cultures and a promoter of humane treatment in the face of the abuses of sometimes unscrupulous colonizers. The denunciation of injustices and abuses through the work of Montesinos, las Casas, Cordoba, Fray Juan del Valle, and so many others was like a cry that led to laws based on acknowledgment of the sacred value of the person. The Christian conscience flourished with prophetic courage in that cathedral of dignity and freedom known as the School of Vitoria at the University of Salamanca (cf. *Speech,* May 14, 1992) and in so many outstanding defenders of the natives in both Spain and Latin America. Their names are well known, and they have been recalled with admiration and gratitude on the occasion of the fifth centenary anniversary.

I myself suggested that an international symposium be held on the history of the evangelization of the Americas, organized by the Pontifical Commission for Latin America, to determine the outlines of historical truth, placing in relief the continent's Christian roots and Catholic identity. The data of history show that a valid, fruitful, and admirable labor of evangelization took place, thereby opening the way to the truth about God and the human being in the Americas—so much so, indeed, that the evangelization itself became a kind of tribunal for holding accountable those responsible for such abuses.

I have been able to witness the fruitfulness of the gospel seed deposited in these blessed lands during the apostolic journeys that the Lord has allowed me to make to your particular churches. How can I fail to show openly my ardent gratitude to God, for I have been allowed to become familiar with the living reality of the Church in Latin America! On my journeys to this continent and on your *ad limina* visits as well as in various other encounters—which have strengthened the bonds of episcopal collegiality and shared responsibility in pastoral care for the whole Church—I have been able to verify many times the vitality of the faith of your ecclesial communities. I have also been able to measure the breadth of the challenges facing the Church, which is inseparably linked to the fate of the peoples of the continent.

5. This general conference is meeting to trace guidelines for an evangelizing activity that will place Christ in the heart and on the lips of all Latin Americans. This is our task: to make the truth about Christ and the truth about the human being penetrate ever more deeply into all strata of society and to transform it (cf. *Speech to the Pontifical Commission for Latin America,* June 14, 1991).

In its deliberations and conclusions, this conference must know how to combine the three doctrinal and pastoral elements that constitute the three axes of the new evangelization: Christology, ecclesiology, and anthropology. The challenges to the Church's evangelizing activity in the Americas today must be met through a deep and solid Christology, and on the basis of a sound anthropology and a clear and correct ecclesiological vision. As a sign of deep communion and shared responsibility for the Church, I now want to share with you some observations along the lines of the conference's main themes that may be of help in your ministry as pastors generously committed to the flock that the Lord has entrusted to you. My intention is to present some doctrinal and pastoral priorities from the standpoint of the new evangelization.

II. NEW EVANGELIZATION

6. The new evangelization is the central idea within the whole set of issues to be addressed in this conference.

Since my meeting in Haiti with the bishops of CELAM in 1983, I have been giving particular emphasis to this expression in order to arouse a new fervor and new concerns for evangelization in the Americas and the whole world, that is, in order to give pastoral work "a fresh forward impulse, capable of creating, with a Church still more firmly rooted in the undying power and strength of Pentecost, a new period of evangelization" (*Evangelii Nuntiandi,* 2).

The new evangelization does not consist in a "new gospel," which would always arise from ourselves, our culture, our analysis of human need. Hence, it would not be "gospel" but mere human invention, and there would be no salvation in it. Nor does it consist of trimming away from the gospel everything that seems difficult for the contemporary mind-set to accept. Culture is not the measure of the gospel; rather Jesus Christ is the measure of all culture and all human endeavor. No, the new evangelization does not arise from the desire "to curry favor with human beings" or to "please people" (Gal 1:10), but from responsibility for the gift that God has made to us in Christ, in which we accede to the truth about God and about the human being, and to the possibility of true life.

The starting point for the new evangelization is the certainty that in Christ are "inscrutable riches" (Eph 3:8) that are not exhausted by any culture or any age and that we human beings can always approach in order to be enriched (cf. *Final Declaration* of the Special Assembly for Europe of the Synod of Bishops, 3). That wealth is first and foremost Christ himself, his person, for he himself is our salvation. By approaching him through faith and being incorporated into his body, which is the Church, we human beings of any period and any culture can find the answer to those ever old and ever new questions with which we human beings face the mystery of our existence and which we bear indelibly engraved in our hearts from creation and from the wound of sin.

7. Newness does not touch the content of the gospel message, which is unchangeable, for Christ is the same "yesterday, today and forever" (Heb 13:8). Hence, the gospel is to be preached with complete faithfulness and purity as it has been guarded and transmitted by the tradition of the Church. To evangelize is to announce a person, who is Christ. Indeed, "there is no true evangelization if the name, the teaching, the life, the promises, the kingdom

and the mystery of Jesus of Nazareth, the Son of God, are not proclaimed" (*Evangelii Nuntiandi,* 22). Hence, reductive Christologies, whose errors I have pointed out on several occasions (cf. *Opening Address,* Puebla Conference [January 28, 1979], I, 4), cannot be accepted as instruments for the new evangelization. When evangelization takes place, the unity of the Church's faith must shine forth not only in the authentic magisterium of the bishops but also in service to truth by pastors of souls, theologians, catechists and all those who are committed to proclaiming and preaching the faith.

In this regard, the Church stimulates, esteems, and respects the vocation of the theologian, whose "role is to pursue in a particular way an ever deeper understanding of the word of God contained in the inspired Scriptures and handed on by the living tradition of the Church" (Congregation for the Doctrine of the Faith, instruction, *On the Ecclesial Vocation of the Theologian* [May 24, 1990], 6). That noble and necessary vocation arises within the Church and presumes that the theologian is a believer and has an attitude of faith to which he or she must bear witness in the community. "The right conscience of the Catholic theologian presumes not only faith in the word of God ... but also love for the Church, from whom he receives his mission, and respect for her divinely assisted magisterium" (ibid., 38). Theology is thus called to provide a great service to the new evangelization.

8. Certainly, it is the truth that makes us free (cf. Jn 8:32). However, we must certainly point out that some positions on what constitutes truth, freedom, and conscience are unacceptable. Some have even gone so far as to justify dissent by invoking "theological pluralism sometimes to the point of a relativism which calls the integrity of the faith into question. [Some think that] the documents of the magisterium reflect nothing more than a debatable theology" (ibid., 34); "in opposition to and in competition with the authentic magisterium, there thus arises a kind of 'parallel magisterium' of theologians" (ibid.). Furthermore, we cannot ignore the fact that "attitudes of general opposition to church teaching which even come to expression in organized groups," contestation and discord, besides "presenting serious harm to the community of the Church," are also an obstacle to evangelization (cf. ibid., 32).

The confession of faith "Jesus Christ yesterday, today, and forever," found in the Letter to the Hebrews—which is, as it were, the backdrop of the topic of this fourth conference—draws our attention to the words of the next verse: "Do not be carried away by all kinds of strange teaching" (Heb 13:9). You, beloved pastors, have to be especially watchful for the faith of simple people lest it be disoriented and confused.

9. All evangelizers must also pay particular attention to catechesis. At the outset of my pontificate, I sought to give new impetus to this pastoral work with the apostolic exhortation *Catechesi Tradendae,* and recently I have approved the *Catechism of the Catholic Church,* which I present as the best gift that the Church can make to its bishops and to the entire people of God. It is a valuable tool for the new evangelization, compiling all the doctrine that the Church must teach.

I likewise trust that the biblical movement will continue to provide its benefits in Latin America and that Sacred Scripture will increasingly nourish the life of the faithful. To that end, it is essential that pastoral agents tirelessly delve more deeply into the word of God, living it and transmitting it to others faithfully, that is, taking into account "the living tradition of the whole Church . . . along with the harmony which exists between elements of the faith" (*Dei Verbum,* 12). Likewise, the liturgical movement must give a renewed impetus to the inner experience of the mysteries of our faith, leading to the encounter with the risen Christ in the Church's liturgy. It is in the celebration of the word and the sacraments, but especially in the eucharist, the apex and source of the Church's life and of all evangelization, that there is effected our saving encounter with Christ, to whom we are mystically united and become his Church (cf. *Lumen Gentium,* 7). Therefore, I exhort you to give a new impetus to the respectful, vital, and participatory celebration of liturgical assemblies, with that profound sense of faith and contemplation of the mysteries of salvation that is so rooted in your peoples.

10. The newness of the evangelizing activity that we have called for is a matter of attitude, style, effort, and planning, or as I proposed in Haiti, of ardor, methods, and expression (cf. *Address* to Bishops of CELAM, March 9, 1983). An evangelization new in its ardor means a solid faith, an intense pastoral charity, and a steadfast fidelity, that under the action of the Spirit generate a spirituality, an irrepressible enthusiasm for the task of announcing the gospel. In New Testament terminology, it is that "parrhesia" that ignites the apostle's heart (cf. Acts 5:28-29; cf. *Redemptoris Missio,* 45). This parrhesia must also be the seal of your apostolate in the Americas. No one can silence you, for you are heralds of truth. The truth of Christ must enlighten your minds and hearts with the active, tireless, and public proclamation of Christian values.

However, the new times demand that the Christian message reach people today through new methods of apostolate and that it be expressed in language and forms that are accessible to Latin Americans, who need Christ and thirst for the gospel. How does one make accessible, penetrating, valid, and deep the response to people today without in any way altering or changing the content of the gospel message? How does one reach the heart of the culture that we want to evangelize? How does one speak of God in a world in which there is a growing process of secularization?

11. As you have indicated in the meetings and conversations that we have held during these years both in Rome and in my visits to your particular churches, today the simple faith of your peoples is being assaulted by secularization, with the consequent weakening of religious and moral values. In urban environments there is a growing cultural tendency to trust only in science and technological progress and to be hostile to faith. Certain "models" of life are pitted against gospel values. Under the pressure of secularism, some even treat faith as though it were a threat to human freedom and autonomy.

Nevertheless, we cannot forget that recent history has demonstrated that when the truth about God and the truth about the human being are denied, under the cover of certain ideologies, it becomes impossible to build a society with a human face. It is to be hoped that the fall of those regimes of so-called real socialism in Eastern Europe will lead people in this continent to realize that the value of such ideologies is ephemeral. The roots of the crisis of Marxist collectivism have not been merely economic, since the truth about the human being is necessarily very closely connected to the truth about God, as I have emphasized in the encyclical *Centesimus Annus* (41).

The new evangelization must therefore be a response that is integral, timely, and flexible, that strengthens the Catholic faith in its fundamental truths and in its individual, family, and societal dimensions.

12. Like the Good Shepherd, you are to feed the flock entrusted to you and defend it from rapacious wolves. A source of division and discord in your ecclesial communities are—as you well know—the sects and "pseudospiritual" movements mentioned in the *Puebla Conclusions* (628), whose aggressiveness and expansion must be faced.

As many of you have pointed out, the advance of the sects highlights a pastoral vacuum, often caused by a lack of formation that leads to the undermining of Christian identity. A further effect is that large masses of Catholics who are without adequate religious attention—among other reasons because of a shortage of priests—are at the mercy of very active sectarian proselytizing campaigns. It may also happen, however, that the faithful do not find in pastoral agents that strong sense of God that such agents should be transmitting in their lives. "Such situations may be the occasion for many poor and simple persons to become easy prey for the sects, as unfortunately is happening. In the sects, they are looking for a religious meaning to life that they perhaps do not find in those who should be abundant examples of it" (apostolic letter, *Los Caminos del Evangelio*, 20).

Moreover, we should not underestimate a particular strategy aimed at weakening the bonds that unite Latin American countries and so to undermine the kinds of strength provided by unity. To that end, significant amounts of money are offered to subsidize proselytizing campaigns that try to shatter such Catholic unity.

The worrisome phenomenon of the sects must be countered with pastoral action centered on the whole person, on his or her communal dimension and yearning for a personal relationship with God. It is a fact that where the Church's presence is dynamic, such as in parishes where there is a steady formation in the word of God; where the liturgy is active and people participate; where there is a solid Marian piety, true solidarity in the social field, a notable pastoral concern for the family, youth, and the sick, we see that the sects or parareligious movements do not become established or do not make progress.

Because of its eminently Catholic roots, the deep-seated popular religiosity of your faithful, with its extraordinary values of faith and piety, of sacrifice and solidarity, when properly evangelized and joyfully celebrated and directed toward the mysteries of Christ and the Virgin Mary, may serve as antidote to the sects and help safeguard fidelity to the message of salvation.

III. HUMAN DEVELOPMENT

13. Since the Church is aware that the human being—not an abstract being, but the concrete human being in history—"is the route that it must traverse in carrying out its mission" (*Redemptor Hominis,* 14), stimulating human development must be the logical outcome of evangelization, which tends toward the comprehensive liberation of the person (cf. *Evangelii Nuntiandi,* 29-39).

When you look at this concrete human being, pastors of the Church, you are well aware how problematic is the current social condition of Latin America, where large segments of the population are poor and excluded. Accordingly, in solidarity with the cry of the poor, you feel called to act as the good Samaritan (cf. Lk 10:25 37), since love for God is shown in love for the human person. The apostle James thus reminds us with those very serious words, "If a brother or sister has nothing to wear and no food for the day, and one of you says to them, 'Go in peace, keep warm and eat well,' but you do not give them the bodily necessities, what good is it?" (Jas 2:15-16).

Concern for the social dimension is "part of the Church's evangelizing mission" (*Sollicitudo Rei Socialis*, 41) and is also "an essential part of the Christian message, since this doctrine points out the direct consequences of that message in the life of society and situates daily work and struggles for justice in the context of bearing witness to Christ the savior" (*Centesimus Annus,* 5).

As Vatican Council II states in the pastoral constitution *Gaudium et Spes,* the problem of human development cannot be considered apart from human relationship with God (cf. nos. 43, 45). Indeed, to pit authentic human development and God's plan for humankind against one another is a grave distortion, the product of a secularistic cast of thought. Genuine efforts at human betterment must always respect the truth about God and the truth about the human being, and respect both God's rights and the rights of the human being.

14. Beloved pastors, you are in close contact with the anguished situation of so many brothers and sisters who lack what is needed for a genuinely human life. Despite progress in some fields, poverty remains a reality and is even increasing. Problems are mounting with the decline in purchasing power of money due to sometimes uncontrolled inflation and deteriorating trade relations, with consequent lower prices paid for certain raw materials and the crushing weight of international debt, whose social consequences are so dreadful. The serious problem of growing unemployment adds to the suffering by preventing people from putting bread on the table and blocking their access to other basic goods (cf. *Laborem Exercens,* 18).

Since I am vividly aware of how serious this situation is, I have continually issued calls for an active, just, and urgent international solidarity. This duty of justice applies to the whole of humankind, but especially to the rich countries, which cannot shirk their responsibility toward developing countries. Such solidarity is a demand of the universal common good that ought to command respect from all members of the human family (cf. *Gaudium et Spes,* 26).

15. The world cannot feel serene and satisfied in the face of the chaotic and disturbing scene we see before us: nations, segments of the population, families, and individuals growing ever richer and more privileged opposite peoples, families, and a vast number of individuals mired in poverty, victims

of hunger and illness who lack decent housing, sanitation, and access to culture. All of that eloquently testifies to a real disorder and an institutionalized injustice. Sometimes it is augmented by delays in taking the required measures, inertia and imprudence, or even the violation of ethical principles in administration, as in the case of corruption. All of this requires "changes of mentality, behavior and structures" (*Centesimus Annus*, 60) so as to bridge the chasm between the rich and poor countries (cf. *Laborem Exercens*, 16; *Centesimus Annus*, 14) as well as the profound differences among citizens of the same country. In short, the new ideal of solidarity must come to prevail over the obsolescent will to dominate.

However, the proposal to resolve the problem by reducing demographic growth without any concern for the morality of the means employed for that purpose is deceptive and unacceptable. The point is not to reduce at any cost the number of those invited to the banquet of life; what is needed is to augment resources and distribute wealth with greater justice so that all may participate equitably in the goods of creation.

Solutions must be sought on a worldwide scale by establishing a true economy of communion and participation in goods on both international and national levels. In that regard, one factor that can make a notable contribution to overcoming the pressing problems today affecting this continent is Latin American integration. Those in charge of governments have a grave responsibility to promote the process—already under way—of integrating peoples whom a common geography, the Christian faith, language and culture have already drawn together in the course of history.

16. In continuity with the Medellín and Puebla conferences, the church reaffirms the preferential option on behalf of the poor. That option is not exclusive or excluding, since the message of salvation is intended for all. It is "an option, moreover, that is based essentially on God's word, and not on criteria provided by human sciences or opposed ideologies, which often reduce the poor to abstract sociopolitical and economic categories. But it is a firm and irrevocable option" (*Address to the Roman Curia* [December 21, 1984], 9).

As the *Puebla Conclusions* says, "When we draw near to the poor in order to accompany them and serve them, we are doing what Christ taught us to do when he became our brother, poor like us. Hence, service to the poor is the privileged, though not the exclusive, gauge of our following of Christ. The best service to our fellows is evangelization, which disposes them to fulfill themselves as children of God, liberates them from injustices, and fosters their integral advancement" (*Puebla Conclusions,* 1145). Such gospel criteria for service to the needy will avoid any temptation toward complicity with those responsible for the causes of poverty or dangerous ideological deviations that are incompatible with the Church's doctrine and mission.

The genuine praxis of liberation must always be inspired by the doctrine of the Church as set forth in the two instructions by the Congregation for the Doctrine of Faith (*Libertatis Nuntius,* 1984; *Libertatis Conscientia,* 1986), which must be kept in mind when the topic of liberation theologies comes up for discussion. However, the Church can in no way allow any ideology or political current to snatch away the banner of justice, for it is one of the primary demands of the gospel and, at the same time, a fruit of the coming of God's kingdom.

17. As the *Puebla Conclusions* already pointed out, some human groups are especially mired in poverty; such is the case of indigenous people (cf. 1265). It has been my intention to deliver a special message expressing solidarity and closeness to them as well as to African Americans. I will give that message tomorrow to a group of representatives of their communities. As a gesture of solidarity, the Holy See has recently created the *Populorum Progressio* Foundation, which has a special fund for small farmers, Indians, and other human groups in the rural sector, who are especially vulnerable in Latin America.

In this same line of pastoral care for the most vulnerable groups of people, this general conference might consider the desirability of celebrating in the near future a meeting of representatives of the episcopacies of the Americas—which might even have a synodal character—in order to increase cooperation among the various local churches in different fields of pastoral action. In the framework of the new evangelization and as an expression of episcopal communion, such a meeting could also deal with issues of justice and solidarity among all the nations of the Americas. On the threshold of the third Christian millennium and after the fall of many ideological barriers and borders, the Church feels that it has an inescapable duty to unite even more closely all the peoples that make up this great continent. It likewise feels that its own religious mission requires it to give impetus to a spirit of solidarity among all of them, particularly in finding ways to solve the dramatic situations of the vast sectors of the population who aspire to a legitimate overall progress and more just and decent living conditions.

18. There is no genuine human development, true liberation, or preferential option for the poor unless it is based on the very foundations of the dignity of the person and of the surroundings in which the person must develop, according to the Creator's design. Hence, among the topics and options that

require the entire attention of the Church, I cannot fail to recall those of the family and of life: two things that are closely interrelated, since the family is "the sanctuary of life" (*Centesimus Annus,* 39). Indeed, "the future of humankind is forged in the family; hence, every person of good will must by all means strive to save and promote family values and requirements" (*Familiaris Consortio,* 86).

Despite the problems now besieging marriage and the institution of the family, it can still serve as the "first and vital cell of society" (*Apostolicam Actuositatem,* 11); it can create great energies that are necessary for the good of humankind. Hence, we must "proclaim with joy and conviction the 'good news' on the family" (*Familiaris Consortio,* 86). That good news must be announced here in Latin America, where alongside the high regard shown for the family, common-law arrangements are unfortunately very widespread. In view of this reality and the growing pressures in favor of divorce, it is necessary to promote adequate measures on behalf of the family core in order to safeguard the stability of the union of life and love within marriage in accordance with God's plan, and a suitable education for the children.

Closely connected to this problem is the serious phenomenon of street children in large Latin American cities, whose lives are sapped by hunger and disease and who are vulnerable and subjected to so many dangers, including drugs and prostitution. Here is yet another issue that must compel your pastoral concern, recalling Jesus' words: "Let the children come to me" (Mt 19:14).

Life, from its conception in the mother's womb until its natural end, must be defended firmly and courageously. There must be created in the Americas a culture of life that can counter the anti-culture of death that threatens to prevail in some nations, as manifested in abortion, euthanasia, war, guerrilla warfare, kidnapping, terrorism, and other forms of violence or exploitation. Within this spectrum of assaults against life, drug trafficking stands at the fore, and those in authority must counter it with all available lawful means.

19. Who will deliver us from these signs of death? The experience of the contemporary world has increasingly demonstrated that ideologies cannot overthrow the evil that holds human beings in bondage. The only one who can free from this evil is Christ. As we celebrate five centuries of evangelization, we turn our gaze with feeling toward that moment of grace when Christ was given to us once and for all. The painful situation of so many of our Latin American sisters and brothers does not lead us to despair. On the contrary, it makes more urgent the task confronting the Church: to reawaken within the heart of each baptized person the grace that has been received. "For this reason I remind you," wrote St. Paul to Timothy, "to stir into flame the gift

of God that you have through the imposition of my hands" (2 Tm 1:6).

Just as the people of the new covenant were born in the acceptance of the Holy Spirit at Pentecost, so only will that acceptance be able to bring forth a people capable of generating renewed and free human beings conscious of their dignity. We cannot forget that comprehensive human advancement is critically important for the development of the peoples of Latin America. For "a people's development does not derive primarily from money, material assistance or technological means, but from the formation of consciences and the gradual maturing of ways of thinking and patterns of behavior. The human being is the principal agent of development, not money or technology" (*Redemptoris Missio,* 58). Latin America's greatest wealth is its peoples. By "awakening their consciences through the gospel," the Church contributes to the awakening of dormant energies that can be put to work in building a new civilization (cf. ibid.).

IV. CHRISTIAN CULTURE

20. Although the gospel is not identified with any particular culture, it certainly should provide cultures with inspiration to transform themselves from within by enriching them with the Christian values that derive from faith. Indeed, the evangelization of cultures represents the deepest and most comprehensive way to evangelize a society, since the message of Christ thereby permeates people's awareness and is projected into the "ethos" of a people, its essential attitudes, its institutions and all its structures (cf. *Address to Medellín Intellectuals and to the University World* [July 5, 1986], 2).

CELAM has devoted considerable study and reflection to the topic of "culture" in recent years. The Church also directs its attention to this important topic "since the new evangelization must be projected toward the 'coming' culture, toward all cultures, including indigenous cultures" (cf. *Angelus,* June 28, 1992). To proclaim Jesus Christ in all cultures is the Church's central concern and the object of its mission. In our time, it demands, first, that cultures be discerned as a human reality to be evangelized and, consequently, the pressing need for a new kind of collaboration among all those responsible for the work of evangelization.

21. In our day, we can see a cultural crisis of unsuspected dimensions. It is true that the existing cultural substratum offers a good number of positive values, many of them the result of evangelization. At the same time, however, it has eliminated fundamental religious values and has introduced deceitful notions that from a Christian standpoint are unacceptable.

The absence of those fundamental Christian values in the culture of modernity has not only obscured the transcendent dimension and inclined many people—even in Latin American—toward religious indifference, but it is also the key reason for the social disillusionment that has given rise to the crisis of that culture. As a result of the autonomy introduced by rationalism, today values tend to be based primarily on a subjective social consensus that often leads to positions contrary even to natural ethics. Consider the drama of abortion, abuses in genetic engineering, and attacks on life and on the dignity of the person.

The plurality of options available today demands that there be a deep pastoral renewal through the gospel discernment of the prevailing values, attitudes, and collective behavior patterns which often are a decisive factor in choosing either good or evil. Our times require special effort and sensitivity in order to inculturate the message of Jesus in such a way that Christian values can transform the various focal points of culture, purifying them if necessary, and making possible the consolidation of a Christian culture that can renew, extend, and unify past and present historic values so as to respond adequately to the challenges of our time (cf. *Redemptoris Missio*, 52). One such challenge to evangelization is that of intensifying the dialogue between the sciences and faith so as to create a true Christian humanism. The point is to show that science and technology help civilize and humanize the world insofar as they are imbued with the wisdom of God. In this regard, I want to encourage actively universities and centers of advanced study, and particularly those that belong to the Church, to renew their efforts in the dialogue between faith and science.

22. The Church views with concern the split existing between gospel values and modern cultures, for these cultures run the risk of turning inward in a kind of agnostic self-enclosure with no reference to the moral dimension (cf. *Address to the Pontifical Council for Culture*, January 18, 1983). In this regard, Pope Paul VI's words retain all their validity: "The rift between the gospel and culture is undoubtedly an unhappy circumstance of our times, just as it has been in other eras. Accordingly, we must devote all our resources and all our efforts to sedulous evangelization of human culture or, rather, of the various human cultures. They must be regenerated through contact with the gospel. But this contact cannot be effected unless the good news is proclaimed" (*Evangelii Nuntiandi*, 20).

The Church, which regards the human being as its "way" (cf. *Redemptor Hominis*, 14), must know how to respond adequately to the present crisis of culture. In response to the complex phenomenon of modernity, there must be generated a cultural alternative that is fully Christian. If true culture expresses the universal values of the person, what can project more light on the situation of human beings, their dignity and purpose, their freedom and destiny than the gospel of Christ?

At this moment, marking a half-millennium of the evangelization of your peoples, I invite you, dear brothers, with the ardor of the new evangelization and animated by the Spirit of Christ, to make the Church present at the cultural crossroads of our time, in order to imbue with Christian values the very roots of the "coming" culture and of all existing cultures. In this regard, you must devote special attention to indigenous and African American cultures, drawing on and highlighting everything that is deeply human and humanizing within them. Their view of life, which acknowledges the sacredness of the human being, their deep respect for nature, and their humility, simplicity, and solidarity are values that must stimulate the effort to carry out a genuine inculturated evangelization, one that also promotes progress and leads always to the adoration of God "in spirit and truth" (Jn 4:23). Acknowledging such values, however, does not exempt you from proclaiming at all times that "Christ is the one savior of all, the only one able to reveal God and lead to God" (*Redemptoris Missio,* 5).

"The evangelization of culture is an effort to understand the mind-sets and attitudes of the contemporary world and to shine the light of the gospel on them. It is the intention to reach all levels of human life in order to make it more worthy" (*Address to the World of Culture,* Lima, May 15, 1988). However, this effort at understanding and shedding light must always be accompanied by the proclamation of the good news (cf. *Redemptoris Missio,* 46). Thus, the gospel's penetration of cultures will not be a mere external adaptation, but a "a profound and all-embracing one, which involves the Christian message and also the Church's reflection and practice" (ibid., 52), and will always respect the characteristics and integrity of the faith.

23. Since communication between persons is an important aspect of the creation of culture, modern mass media are extremely important in this regard. It must certainly be one of your priorities to intensify the Church's presence in the world of the media. I am reminded of the ominous words of my venerated predecessor, Pope Paul VI: "The Church would feel guilty before God if she did not avail herself of those powerful instruments that human skill is constantly developing and perfecting" (*Evangelii Nuntiandi,* 45).

Care must be taken, however, in the use of the media for religious education and the spread of religious culture. This responsibility weighs particularly on publishing houses sponsored by Catholic institutions. They ought "to be the object of particular concern for local ordinaries so that their publications always conform to church teaching and make an effective contribution to the good of souls" (Congregation for the Doctrine of the Faith, instruction, *On Some Aspects of the Use of the Instruments of Social Communication in Promoting the Doctrine of the Faith* [March 30, 1992], 15, 2).

Certain social and cultural phenomena emerging to defend human beings and their environment also represent the inculturation of the gospel, and they are to be illuminated by the light of faith. Such is the case of the ecology movement, which advocates according nature its due respect and opposes the disordered exploitation of resources that leads to a deteriorating quality of life. The conviction that "God intended the earth and all that it contains for the use of every human being and people" (*Gaudium et Spes,* 69) must be the inspiration for a system for using resources that is more just and better coordinated on a worldwide scale. The Church endorses concern for the environment and urges governments to protect this inheritance according to the criteria of the common good (cf. *25th World Day of Peace Message,* January 1, 1992).

24. The challenge represented by the "coming" culture does not weaken our hope, however, and we thank God that in Latin America, the gift of Catholic faith has reached very deeply into its peoples, shaping the Christian soul of the continent during these five hundred years and inspiring many of its institutions. The Church in Latin America has indeed been able to make its way into the culture of the people and has known how to place the gospel message at the basis of its thinking, its fundamental principles of life, its criteria for judgment, and its norms for activity.

We now face the formidable challenge of the ongoing inculturation of the gospel in your peoples, a topic that you must take up clearsightedly and in depth during the next few days. Latin America provides an example of a perfectly inculturated evangelization in St. Mary of Guadalupe. Certainly, since the beginning of the Christianization of the New World in the light of the gospel of Jesus, genuine indigenous cultural values have been incarnated in the figure of Mary. In the *mestizo* face of the Virgin of Tepeyac is summed up the great principle of inculturation: the deep transformation of genuine cultural values through their integration into Christianity and the rooting of Christianity in the various cultures (cf. *Redemptoris Missio,* 52).

V. A NEW ERA UNDER THE SIGN OF HOPE

25. These then, beloved brothers and sisters, are some of the challenges facing the Church at this moment of new evangelization. Faced with this panorama full of questions but also full of promise, we must ask ourselves what path the Church in Latin America must follow so that in this next stage of its history its mission may produce the fruits that the Lord of the harvest expects (cf. Lk 10:2; Mk 4:20). Your assembly must sketch the countenance of a living and dynamic Church growing in faith, becoming holier, loving, suffering, committing itself and awaiting its Lord, as we are reminded by Vatican II, which is an obligatory reference point in the life and mission of every pastor (cf. *Gaudium et Spes,* 2).

A difficult task awaits you during the next few days, but it is marked by the sign of hope that comes from the risen Christ. It is your mission to be heralds of hope, as the apostle Peter tells us (cf. 1 Pt 3:15). That hope is based on God's promises, in fidelity to his word, and its unshakable certainty is Christ's resurrection, his ultimate victory over sin and death, the primary proclamation and the root of all evangelization, the foundation for all promotion of human development, the principle of all genuine Christian culture, which can only be the culture of resurrection and life enlivened by the breath of the Spirit of Pentecost.

Beloved brothers in the episcopacy, in the unity of the local Church, which springs from the eucharist, is found the whole episcopal college with Peter's successor at its head, as something that belongs to the very essence of the local church (cf. Congregation for the Doctrine of the Faith, *Letter to Bishops on Some Aspects of the Church Understood as Communion,* 14). Parishes and Christian communities are to flourish around the bishop and in perfect communion with him like vigorous cells of diocesan life. Therefore the new evangelization demands that the whole life of the diocese be renewed. Parishes, apostolic movements, associations of the faithful and all ecclesial communities in general must always be evangelized and evangelizing. Basic Christian communities in particular must always be characterized by a decisive universal and missionary thrust that instills in them a renewed apostolic dynamism (cf. *Evangelii Nuntiandi,* 58; *Puebla Conclusions,* 640-642). These communities must be stamped with a clear ecclesial identity and find in the eucharist, presided over by a priest, the center of their life and communion among their members, in close union with their pastors and full harmony with the Church's magisterium.

26. An indispensable condition for the new evangelization is that there be

many qualified evangelizers available. Hence, the promotion of priestly and religious vocations as well as those of other pastoral agents must be a priority for bishops and a commitment for the whole people of God. Throughout Latin America, vocational pastoral work must be given a decided impetus, and issues concerning seminaries and training centers for men and women religious must be faced, along with the problem of ongoing training for the clergy and a better distribution of priests among the various local churches, and especially now, the valuable work of permanent deacons. There are appropriate guidelines for all of this in my postsynodal apostolic exhortation, *Pastores Dabo Vobis.*

With regard to men and women religious, who carry the burden of a good deal of the pastoral work in Latin America, I want to mention the apostolic letter *Los Caminos del Evangelio,* which I addressed to them June 29, 1990. Here, I would also like to recall secular institutes, with their dynamic vitality in the midst of the world, and the members of societies of apostolic life, which carry out a vast missionary activity.

Today, the members of religious congregations, both male and female, must be more centered on work that is specifically evangelizing, unfolding the whole wealth of pastoral initiatives and tasks that flow from their various charisms. Faithful to their founders, they must be characterized by a deep sense of church and a witness of close and faithful collaboration in pastoral activity, which is to be under the leadership of diocesan ordinaries, and in particular aspects, of bishops' conferences.

As I recalled in my *Letter to Contemplative Women in Latin America* (December 12, 1989), the Church's evangelizing activity is sustained by such sanctuaries of the contemplative life, which are so numerous throughout the continent. They give witness to the radical nature of consecration to God, which must always be in the forefront of our options.

27. In my postsynodal apostolic exhortation *Christifideles Laici,* on the calling and mission of lay people in the Church, I especially wanted to emphasize that in the "grand, demanding and splendid enterprise" of the new evangelization, the work of lay people, and particularly catechists and "delegates of the word," is indispensable. The Church expects a great deal of all those lay people who, enthusiastically and with the efficacy of the gospel, are involved through the new apostolic movements. Those movements, which reflect the need for a greater presence of the faith in the life of society, must be coordinated by means of overall pastoral planning. At this moment, when I have invited all to work with apostolic zeal in the vineyard of the Lord,

without excluding anyone, "lay faithful must feel that they play a vital and responsible role in this enterprise (new evangelization), called as they are to proclaim and live the gospel by serving the values and demands of people and society" (no. 64). The Latin American woman, who passes on the faith, is worthy of all praise. Her role in the Church and in society must be properly highlighted (cf. apostolic letter, *Mulieris Dignitatem*). Special pastoral concern should be devoted to the sick, bearing in mind the evangelizing power of suffering (cf. apostolic letter, *Salvifici Doloris*, February 11, 1984).

I issue a special call to the youth of Latin America. They—who are so numerous on a continent that is young—will be the protagonists in the life of society and of the Church in the new Christian millennium that is now upon us. The beauty of the Christian calling must be presented to them in their own language, and they must be offered high and noble ideals that can sustain them in their aspirations for a more just and familial society.

28. All are called to build the civilization of love on this continent of hope. Furthermore, Latin America, which has received the faith transmitted by the churches of the Old World, must prepare to spread Christ's message around the world "out of its poverty" (cf. *Messages to the Third and Fourth Latin American Missionary Congresses,* Santa Fe de Bogota [1987] and Lima [1991]). "The moment has come to commit all of the Church's energies to the new evangelization and to the mission *ad gentes.* No believer in Christ, no institution of the Church, can avoid this supreme duty: to proclaim Christ to all peoples" (*Redemptoris Missio,* 3). This moment has also come for Latin America. "Faith is strengthened when it is given to others! The new evangelization of Christian peoples," and in the churches of the Americas, "will find inspiration and support in commitment to the Church's universal mission" (ibid., 2). The greatest sign of gratitude for receiving Christ five hundred years ago and the greatest sign of its Christian vitality is to become committed to mission.

29. Beloved brothers in the episcopacy, as successors of the apostles, you must devote your tireless endeavors to the flock "of which the Holy Spirit has appointed you overseers, in which you tend the Church of God" (Acts 20:28). Moreover, as members of the episcopal college, in true, close, and heartfelt unity with Peter's successor, you are called to maintain communion with and concern for the whole Church. On this occasion, as members of the Fourth General Conference of the Latin American Episcopate, you bear a historic responsibility.

By virtue of faith, the revealed word, the action of the Spirit and through the eucharist over which the bishop presides, the local church has a special relationship of mutual interiority with the universal Church, for in it is present and truly operating the Church of Christ, which is one, holy, catholic, and apostolic (cf. *Christus Dominus,* 11). In it must shine forth that holiness of life to which every evangelizer is called; it must give witness to an intense experience of the mystery of Jesus Christ, which is strongly felt and sensed in the eucharist, in steadfast listening to the word, in prayer, in sacrifice, in generous surrender to the Lord, which in priests and other consecrated persons is given a special expression in celibacy.

We must not forget that the primary form of evangelization is witness (cf. *Redemptoris Missio,* 42-43), that is, proclaiming the message of salvation through one's works and the consistency of one's life, thus making it incarnate in the everyday history of human beings. From its origins, the Church became present and operative not only through the explicit proclamation of the gospel of Christ, but also and above all through the radiance of Christian life. Hence, the new evangelization requires a consistency of life, a dense witness of charity under the sign of unity, in order that the world may believe (cf. Jn 17:23).

30. Jesus Christ, the faithful witness, the pastor of the pastors, is in our midst, for we have gathered in his name (cf. Mt 1:20). With us is the Spirit of the Lord, who guides the Church to the fullness of truth and rejuvenates it with the revealed word, as in a new Pentecost.

In the communion of saints, a vast array of Latin American saints is watching over the labors of this important ecclesial encounter. They evangelized this continent with their word and their virtues, and many of them made it fruitful with their blood. They are the supreme fruits of evangelization.

As she did in the upper room of Pentecost, the mother of Jesus and mother of the Church is with us. Her affectionate presence in every corner of Latin America and in the hearts of her children is the assurance of the prophetic thrust and gospel zeal that must accompany your labors.

31. "Blessed are you who believed that what was spoken to you by the Lord would be fulfilled"(Lk 1:45). These words that Elizabeth addresses to Mary, who is bearing Christ, are applicable to the Church, of which the mother of the Redeemer is type and model. Blessed are you, Americas, Church of the Americas, who also bear Christ, you have received the proclamation of salvation and have believed "what was spoken to you by the Lord!"The faith is your joy, the source of your happiness. Blessed are you, men and women

of Latin America, adults and young people who have known the Redeemer. You can say along with the Church and with Mary that the Lord "has looked upon his handmaid's lowliness" (Lk 1:48). Blessed are you, poor of the earth, for the kingdom of God has come to you!

"What was spoken to you by the Lord will be fulfilled." Be faithful to your baptism. In this celebration of centuries, stir up again the enormous grace you have received. Turn your heart and your gaze back to the center, the source, to him who is the foundation of all happiness, the fullness of all. Open up to Christ, receive the Spirit, so that in all your communities a new Pentecost may take place! And from you will emerge a new and joyful humanity, and you will again experience the power of the Lord's right arm, and "what was spoken to you by the Lord will be fulfilled." What he has told you, Americas, is his love for you, his love for your men and women, for your families, your peoples. And that love will be fulfilled in you, and you will again find yourself, you will find your own countenance; "all ages will call you blessed" (Lk 1:48).

Church of the Americas, today the Lord is passing alongside you. He calls you. In this moment of grace, say your name once more, renew his covenant with you. If only you would listen to his voice so that you may know true and complete joy, and enter into your rest (cf. Ps 94:7,11)!

Let us conclude by calling on Mary, star of the first and of the new evangelization. To her, who always hoped, we entrust our hope. In her hands, we place our pastoral concerns and all the tasks of this conference, entrusting to her mother's heart its success and its projection into the future of the continent. May she help us to proclaim her Son:

"Jesus Christ . . . yesterday, today, and forever!"
Amen.

FOREWORD

We are happy to fulfill our duty of presenting the Santo Domingo document to God's pilgrim people in Latin America and the Caribbean. It is the hope-giving fruit of the Fourth General Conference of Latin American Bishops held last October.

This conference, convoked, inaugurated, and presided over by our Holy Father, John Paul II, labored in warm and deep communion with the vicar of Christ. His opening address was the basic reference point and convergence point for the pastors who took part. It is fitting to observe that this fourth conference was held thirty-seven years after Rio de Janeiro, twenty-four after Medellín, and thirteen after Puebla.

The pastors who gathered in Santo Domingo have drawn together and brought up to date the rich legacy of the past at a wonderful moment: as the first five hundred years of the evangelization of the continent are being commemorated, and as one millennium of Christianity is drawing to a close and another is beginning. It is also a moment when our peoples have been harshly battered by a number of problems and are yearning for a word of hope from the Church.

That is what the Santo Domingo document seeks to be: a word of hope. It is also intended to be an effective instrument for a new evangelization, and a renewed message of Jesus Christ, who is the foundation for human development, and principle of an authentic Christian culture.

The *Santo Domingo Conclusions* are not the result of hasty improvisation. They must be read in the light of the three issue areas indicated by the Holy Father and as the outgrowth of a long and fruitful preparation, which is documented in the contributions made by the bishops' conferences and in a number of books published by the Consejo Episcopal Latinoamericano (CELAM).

Other important documents are published here along with the *Santo Domingo Conclusions*:

- the Holy Father's opening address and his letter authorizing the publication of the document;
- messages from the pope to indigenous people and to African Americans; and
- the message of the fourth conference to the peoples of Latin America and the Caribbean.

In its revision of the text prepared in Santo Domingo, the Holy See has introduced only a few stylistic corrections and some brief editing changes for the sake of clarification.

This new pastoral tool, which contains the elements for a comprehensive evangelization plan, is now in the hands of the bishops' conferences and the local Churches of the Americas. In it, they will be able to find the challenges and pastoral directions most applicable to their specific needs.

May Mary, Mother of the Church and queen of our continent, shed light on the journey that our American continent is now undertaking toward a new evangelization, which is to be projected into greater commitment to comprehensive human development, and is to permeate the cultures of Latin American peoples with the light of the gospel.

+ NICOLAS DE JESUS CARDINAL LOPEZ RODRIGUEZ
   Metropolitan Archbishop of Santo Domingo
   and Primate of the Americas
   President of CELAM

+ JUAN JESUS CARDINAL POSADAS OCAMPO
   Archbishop of Guadalajara
   First Vice-President of CELAM

+ TULIO MANUEL CHIRIVELLA VARELA
   Archbishop of Barquisimeto
   Second Vice-President of CELAM

+ OSCAR ANDRES RODRIGUEZ MARADIAGA, SDB
   Auxiliary Bishop of Tegucigalpa
   President of the CELAM Economic Committee

+ RAYMONDO DAMASCENO ASSIS
   Auxiliary Bishop of Brasilia
   Secretary General of CELAM

Santafé de Bogotá
November 22, 1992
Feast of Jesus Christ, King of the Universe

MESSAGE OF THE FOURTH GENERAL CONFERENCE TO THE PEOPLES OF LATIN AMERICA AND THE CARIBBEAN

I. INTRODUCTION

1. Summoned by the Holy Father John Paul II to the Fourth General Conference of the Latin American Episcopate, which he inaugurated, we, the representatives of the episcopates of Latin America and the Caribbean and the pope's collaborators in the Roman Curia, gathered in Santo Domingo. Bishops from other parts of the world also took part as did priests, deacons, religious, and lay people as well as observers from other Christian churches.

2. An important historic date suggested the fourth conference: the five-hundredth anniversary of the beginning of the evangelization of the New World. Since that time the word of God has made the cultures of our people fruitful and has become an integral part of their history. Therefore, through a lengthy preparation that included a novena of years which the Holy Father inaugurated here in Santo Domingo, we have come together with this spirit of the pope's, that is, in the humility of truth, giving thanks to God for the many great lights and asking his forgiveness for the undeniable shadows that have darkened this period.

3. The Fourth General Conference of the Latin American Episcopate has sought to provide a basic outline for a new impetus to evangelization that will put Christ into the hearts, on the lips, and in the activities and lives of all Latin Americans. Our task is to ensure that the truth about Christ, the Church, and humanity penetrates the strata of society ever more deeply, seeking its gradual transformation. Our work has mainly focused on the new evangelization.

4. Our meeting is closely related to and in continuity with those of the same kind that preceded it: the first was held in Rio de Janeiro, Brazil, in 1955; the second in Medellín, Colombia, in 1968; and the third in Puebla, Mexico, in 1979. We fully confirm the same choices that marked those meetings and embody their more substantive conclusions.

5. These events were a valuable ecclesial experience which has led to a rich episcopal teaching that is useful to the churches and the society of our continent. We now add to these guidelines the commitment to evangelize, which emerges from this meeting, and which we humbly and joyfully offer to our peoples.

6. The motherly presence of Our Lady, inseparably united to the Christian faith in Latin America and the Caribbean, has always been our guide on the path of faith, and especially at this time it sustains us in our work and encourages us in the face of today's pastoral challenges.

II. LATIN AMERICA AND THE CARIBBEAN
BETWEEN FEAR AND HOPE

7. The great majority of our peoples live in critical conditions. We come across this daily in the apostolate and we have expressed it clearly in many documents. Therefore, when we are overwhelmed with grief, God's words to Moses echo in our ears: "I have witnessed the affliction of my people in Egypt and have heard their cry of complaint against their slave drivers, so I know well what they are suffering. Therefore I have come down to rescue them from the hands of the Egyptians and lead them out of that land into a good and spacious land" (Ex 3:7-8).

8. This plight could jeopardize our hope. However, the Holy Spirit's action gives us a vigorous and solid motive for hope: faith in Jesus Christ, who died and is risen, who keeps his promise to be with us always (cf. Mt 28:20). This faith shows him to us as attentive and solicitous to all human need. We seek to carry out what the Son teaches: to assume the pain of humanity and to strive to convert it into the way of redemption.

9. Our hope would be in vain if it were not active and effective. Jesus' message would be a fallacy if there were a division between faith and action. We urge those who are suffering to open their hearts to the message of Jesus, who has the power to give new meaning to their lives and suffering. Faith, combined with hope and charity in the exercise of

apostolic activity, should be transplanted in a "good and spacious land" for those who are suffering today in Latin America and the Caribbean.

10. The present time reminds us of the gospel episode of the paralytic, who had lain sick for thirty-eight years near the pool that could cure him, without anyone helping him into the water. Our task of evangelization aims at putting into practice Jesus' words to the sick man: "Pick up your mat and walk" (Jn 5:1-8).

11. We wish to convert our desire to evangelize into concrete action that makes it possible for people to overcome their problems and recover from their pain—to pick up their mats and walk—and to have primary responsibility for their own lives through their saving encounter with the Lord.

III. HOPE CONVERTED INTO MISSION

1. The New Evangelization

12. Since the Holy Father's visit to Haiti in 1983, we have felt inspired to conduct a renewed, more effective pastoral activity in our individual churches. The name "new evangelization" has been given to this global project that looks forward to a new Pentecost (cf. John Paul II, *Opening Address*, 6-7).

13. St. Luke's account of the disciples on the road to Emmaus shows us the risen Jesus proclaiming the good news. It can be a model for the new evangelization.

2. Jesus Christ Yesterday, Today and Forever: Jesus Reaches Out to Pilgrim Humanity (Lk 24:13-17)

14. While the sad and bewildered disciples of Emmaus were on their way back to their village, the Master drew near to accompany them on their way. Jesus seeks people and accompanies them in order to assume their joys, hopes, hardships, and sadness.

15. Today, too, as pastors of the Church in Latin America and the Caribbean, in fidelity to our divine Master, we wish to renew his spirit of closeness and support for all our brothers and sisters; we proclaim the value and dignity of each person and intend to shed the light of faith on their history

and their daily journey. This is a basic element of the new evangelization.

3. *Human Development: Jesus Walks with People (Lk 24:17-24)*

16. Jesus not only draws near to those on their way. He goes farther: He becomes the way for them (cf. Jn 14:6) and penetrates the depth of their existence, feelings, and behavior. Through simple and direct dialogue, he gets to know their immediate concerns. The same risen Christ accompanied the steps, aspirations and searching, the problems and hardships of his disciples as they went back to their village.

17. Here, Jesus put into practice with his disciples what he had taught a lawyer one day: The wounds and the groans of the dying man lying by the wayside are the urgent problems on our own way (cf. Lk 10:25-37). The parable of the Good Samaritan concerns us directly as it regards all our brothers and sisters, especially sinners for whom Jesus shed his blood. Let us remember in particular those who are suffering: the sick, the elderly who live in solitude, and abandoned children. Let us also look at those who are the victims of injustice: the marginalized; the poor; inhabitants of the slums of great cities; indigenous people and African Americans; farm workers; those without land or work or home; women whose rights are not recognized. Other forms of oppression also make demands on us: violence; pornography; drug trafficking and abuse; terrorism; kidnapping; and many other acute problems.

4. *Culture: Jesus Enlightens Humanity's Way through the Scriptures (Lk 24:25-28)*

18. The Lord's presence does not end in mere human solidarity. The inner drama of the two travelers was that they had lost all hope. This despair was dispelled by explaining the Bible; the good news that they heard from Jesus passed on the message he had received from his Father.

19. Explaining the Scriptures to them, Jesus corrected the errors of a purely temporal messianism and of all those ideologies which enslave humanity. Explaining the Scriptures to them, he clarified their situation and opened up vistas of hope to them.

20. The road Jesus took with his disciples bore the imprint of God's plan for all his creatures and for human existence.

21. We urge all pastoral workers to deepen their study and meditation on

God's word in order to live it and faithfully hand it on to others.

22. We reaffirm the need to find new methods so that those who shape a pluralistic society may fulfil the gospel's ethical demands, above all those of the social order. The Church's social doctrine is an essential part of the Christian message. Its teaching, spread, deepening. and application are necessary requirements for the new evangelization of our peoples.

5. *New Enthusiasm: Jesus Makes Himself Known in the Breaking of the Bread (Lk 24:28-32)*

23. The scriptural explanation, however, was not sufficient to open their eyes and make them see reality from the faith perspective. Doubtless it moved them deeply, but the ultimate gesture by which they could recognize him as living and risen from the dead was the concrete sign of breaking bread.

24. At Emmaus, moreover, a home was opened up for the pilgrim. Christ revealed his intimacy to his traveling companions, and in the act of sharing they recognized the one who throughout his life had given himself to his brothers and sisters and sealed the gift of his whole life with his own death on the cross.

25. At the end of these days of prayer and reflection, we return to the homes which form our particular churches to share with our brothers and sisters, especially those who participate most closely in our ministry: our priests and our deacons, to whom we wish to express special affection and gratitude. May the celebration of the eucharist increasingly enflame their hearts to put into practice the new evangelization, human development, and Christian culture.

6. *Mission: Jesus Is Proclaimed by the Disciples (Lk 24:33-35)*

26. The meeting between the Master and the disciples was over. Jesus disappeared from their sight. Spurred on by fresh enthusiasm, they joyfully set out on their missionary task. They left the village and went to find the other disciples. An experience of faith finds expression in community. Therefore, the disciples went back to Jerusalem to meet their brothers and sisters and tell them how they had met the Lord. On the basis of faith lived in a community, they became preachers of a totally new reality: "The Lord is risen and is again among us." Faith in Jesus of itself implies mission.

27. "For Latin America (and the Caribbean) which received Christ five

hundred years ago, the greatest mark of its appreciation for the gift it has been given and of its Christian vitality is to be committed to missionary activity (*Opening Address*, 28) within and beyond its frontiers.

IV. PASTORAL PRIORITIES

28. With great hope, and taking into account the significant contributions received from the bishops conferences and many other church organizations, the Fourth General Conference proposes the following guidelines for pastoral activity. To undertake our work, we were given direction and support by the Holy Father, who for a long time had been encouraging this conference.

29. First of all, we declare that the Church in Latin America and the Caribbean adheres in faith to Jesus Christ, the same yesterday, today, and forever (cf. Heb 13:8).

30. So that Christ may be the center of our people's life, we call all the faithful to a new evangelization and appeal especially to the laity, and particularly the young people among them. At this moment, we hope that many young people, supported by effective vocational guidance, may respond to the Lord's call to the priesthood and the consecrated life.

   - A renewed catechesis and a living liturgy in a Church constantly concerned with mission will increasingly attract and sanctify all Christians, particularly those who are distant and indifferent to the Church.

   - The new evangelization will intensify the missionary apostolate in all our churches and will make us feel responsible for going beyond our frontiers to bring to other peoples the faith that reached us five hundred years ago.

31. As an expression of the new evangelization, we also commit ourselves to working for the integral development of the Latin American and Caribbean peoples, with the poor as our main concern.

   - In this human development, the family, where life originates, will occupy a privileged and fundamental place. Today it is urgently necessary to promote and protect life from the many attacks upon it from various sectors of modern society.

32. We should promote an evangelization that penetrates to the deepest roots of our peoples' common culture, paying special attention to the growing urban culture.

   - We have devoted particular attention to an authentic incarnation of the gospel in the indigenous and African American cultures of our continent.

   - For this inculturation of the gospel, effective educational programs and the use of the modern means of communications are most important.

V. GREETINGS AND GOOD WISHES

33. We do not wish to conclude this message without addressing an affectionate word to some of the people and groups who have a special place in the Church or in society.

34. Our special greetings go to our priests and deacons, our dedicated coworkers in the episcopal mission, who have been present every day in our thoughts and prayer. We sincerely hope that, as always, they will help us to communicate the conclusions of this conference to the people of our particular churches. We assure them of our paternal and fraternal affection and our gratitude for their devoted, tireless commitment to the ministry.

35. With the same solicitude, let us remember the men and women religious, the members of secular institutes, pastoral workers, catechists, community leaders, members of basic ecclesial communities and ecclesial movements, and the extraordinary ministers, who will certainly draw renewed enthusiasm for their ecclesial work from the conclusions of this conference.

36. Our grateful thoughts are turned to the many missionaries who have proclaimed the gospel on our continent from the very beginning, in conditions of great hardship and with many sacrifices, even to the extent of offering their lives.

37. The presence at our meeting of observers from sister Christian churches gave us encouragement and joy. To them, and through them to all those churches with whom we share faith in Jesus Christ the savior, we offer our fraternal greeting and our prayer that, when God wishes it, we may

fulfill the spiritual testament of Jesus Christ: "That all may be one ... that the world may believe" (Jn 17:21).

38. To the indigenous peoples, the original inhabitants of these lands, the bearers of a host of cultural riches that are the basis of our present culture, and to the descendants of thousands of families from various regions of Africa, we express our respect and the desire to serve them as ministers of the gospel of our Lord Jesus Christ.

39. We are united with the builders and leaders of society—governors, legislators, magistrates, political and military leaders, educators, business people, trade union leaders, and many others—and all peoples of good will who work to promote and protect life in raising the dignity of men and women, in safeguarding their rights, and in seeking and guaranteeing peace far from any form of arms race. From this conference, we exhort them in the exercise of their respective missions to be committed to the service of the people on behalf of justice, solidarity, and integral development, guided by indispensable ethical principles in their decisions.

40. We would like the teaching we impart on the Lord's behalf to be echoed in the families of Latin America and the Caribbean. We ask them, the sanctuaries of life, to sow the seed of the gospel in the hearts of their children through a proper upbringing. At a time when the culture of death threatens us, they will find here a source "that will become a fountain within [them], leaping up to provide eternal life." Through their example and their words, parents are the great evangelizers of the "domestic church," and whether or not this Santo Domingo Conference bears fruit depends to a great extent on them. That is why, together with our greetings, we want to express our closeness and support to them.

41. We urge representatives of the world of culture to intensify their efforts to foster education, the master key to the future. The soul of social dynamism, it is the right and the duty of all to lay the foundations for an authentic integral humanism (cf. John Paul II, *Mass at the Columbus Lighthouse,* 7).

42. We cordially invite all those who work in social communications to make themselves the tireless spokesmen of reconciliation, the steadfast promoters of human and Christian values, and to inspire hope, peace, and solidarity among peoples.

VI. CONCLUSION

43. Full of confidence, therefore, we entrust this message to the people of God in Latin America and the Caribbean. With the same sentiments we offer it to all men and women, especially to the young people of the continent, called to be actively involved in the life of society and the Church in the new Christian millennium already at the door. We offer it also to those who, although they do not share our Christian, Catholic faith, adhere to the message of this Santo Domingo assembly and recognize its call to the Christian and gospel humanism that they respect and live.

44. To our brothers and sisters in the faith, this message is intended to be an explicit profession of faith in Jesus Christ and his good news. In this Jesus, who is the same "yesterday, today, and forever" (Heb 13:8), we have the certitude of finding inspiration, light, and strength for a fresh spirit of evangelization. In him are also found the motives and directions for new efforts toward the authentic human development of nearly 500 million Latin Americans. He will always help us to give our people's cultural values a Christian mark, identity, and the wealth coming from unity in diversity.

45. We would like to propose to everyone the conclusions of the Santo Domingo Conference as a premise for the continued rejuvenation of our predecessors' ideal of the "Great Homeland." We are convinced that the Christian and Catholic roots which our countries have in common will serve as the basis for the unity Latin America desires.

46. There are very active seeds of division in America. This American land is far from being the united continent we desire. Now, besides its primarily religious objective, the new evangelization launched by the Fourth General Conference offers the necessary elements for the birth of the Great Homeland:

    -   The indispensable **reconciliation** whereby, in the logic of the Our Father, past and present divisions will be healed, former and recent injustices will be mutually forgiven, past and present offenses will be forgiven and peace will be restored.

    -   **Solidarity**, people helping others to bear their burden and sharing with them their own aspirations: "The new ideal of solidarity must prevail over the old desire to control" (*Opening Address,* 15).

    -   To achieve the **integration** of our countries the barriers of isolation, discrimination, and mutual indifference must be overcome: "Latin American integration is a factor which can significantly help in overcoming the pressing problems which affect the continent today" (*Opening Address,* 15, 17).

-   Deep **communion** in the Church concerning the political will for progress and well-being.

47. The social and spiritual heritage contained in these four key words— **reconciliation**, **solidarity**, **integration**, and **communion**—could be transformed into Latin America's greatest resource. These are the wishes and prayers of the bishops of the Fourth General Conference of the Latin American Episcopate. It is also the best gift that God's grace could grant us. We think that this heritage is the task and duty of one and all.

48. We entrust our work to Our Lady of Guadalupe, Star of the New Evangelization. She has walked with our peoples from the very first proclamation of Christ. We implore her today to enflame our hearts in order to proclaim, with new methods and new expressions, that Jesus Christ is the same "yesterday, today, and forever" (Heb 13:8).

CONCLUSIONS

New Evangelization

Human Development

Christian Culture

"Jesus Christ . . . the same yesterday, today, and forever"
(Heb 13:8)

ABBREVIATIONS

AA   *Apostolicam Actuositatem,* Vatican Council II, *Decree on the Apostolate of the Laity*

AG   *Ad Gentes,* Vatican Council II, *Decree on the Missionary Activity of the Church*

CA   *Centesisimus Annus,* John Paul II, encyclical letter *On the Hundredth Anniversary of Rerum Novarum* (1991)

CD   *Christus Dominus,* Vatican Council II, *Decree on the Bishops' Pastoral Office in the Church*

CELAM   Consejo Episcopal Latinoamericano—Latin American Bishops Conference

CIC   *Codex Iuris Canonici, Code of Canon Law* (Revised 1983)

CT   *Catechesi Tradendae,* John Paul II, apostolic exhortation *On Catechesis in Our Time* (1979)

CL   *Christifideles Laici,* John Paul II, post-synodal apostolic exhortation *On the Vocation and the Mission of the Lay Faithful in the Church and in the World* (1988)

EN   *Evangelii Nuntiandi,* Paul VI, apostolic exhortation *On Evangelization in the Modern World* (1975)

FC   *Familiaris Consortio,* John Paul II, apostolic exhortation *On the Family* (1981)

GS   *Gaudium et Spes,* Vatican II, *Pastoral Constitution on the Church in the Modern World*

LE   *Laborem Exercens,* John Paul II, encyclical *On Human Work* (1981)

LG   *Lumen Gentium,* Vatican II, *Dogmatic Constitution on the Church*

MD *Mulieris Dignitatem*, John Paul II apostolic letter *On the Dignity and Vocation of Women* (1988)

OA John Paul II, *Opening Address,* to bishops in Santo Domingo, October 12, 1992.

OT *Optatam Totius,* Vatican II, *Decree on Priestly Formation*

PC *Perfectae Caritatis,* Vatican II, *Decree on the Appropriate Renewal of the Religious Life*

PDV *Pastores Dabo Vobis,* John Paul II, post-synodal apostolic exhortation *I Will Give You Shepherds* (1992)

PP *Populorum Progressio,* Paul VI, encyclical *On the Development of Peoples* (1967)

RM *Redemptoris Missio,* John Paul II encyclical letter *On the Permanent Validity of the Church's Missionary Mandate* (1990)

SC *Sacrosanctum Concilium,* Vatican II, *Constitution on the Sacred Liturgy*

SRS *Sollicitudo Rei Socialis*, John Paul II encyclical letter *On Social Concern* (1987)

UR *Unitatis Redintegratio,* Vatican II, *Decree on Ecumenism*

Part I

JESUS CHRIST
GOSPEL OF
THE FATHER

Called together by Pope John Paul II and under the impulse of the Spirit of God   **1**
our Father, we bishops participating in the Fourth General Conference of the
Latin American Episcopates, in continuity with earlier such meetings in Rio
de Janeiro, Medellín, and Puebla, proclaim our faith and our love for Jesus
Christ. He is the same "yesterday, today, and forever" (Heb 13:8).

Gathered together in a new upper room, as it were, around Mary, the Mother
of Jesus, we thank God for the priceless gift of faith and for the countless gifts
of his mercy. We ask forgiveness for being unfaithful to his kindness.
Encouraged by the Holy Spirit, we are preparing to set in motion with new
ardor a new evangelization, one that is to issue in a greater commitment to
comprehensive human development and permeate the cultures of Latin
American peoples with the light of the gospel. It is the Spirit who must give
us the wisdom to discover the new methods and new expressions that may
make the one gospel of Jesus Christ more comprehensible to our brothers and
sisters today and thereby to respond to new questions.

As we consider with the eyes of faith the implanting of the cross of Christ on   **2**
this continent five centuries ago, we understand that it was he, the Lord of
history, who extended the proclamation of salvation to inconceivable proportions. The family of God grew, and the number of those who give thanks
multiplied to the glory of God (cf. 2 Cor 4:15; OA 3). God chose for himself
a new people among the inhabitants of these lands. Although they were
unknown to the old world, they were well "known to God from all eternity, and
he had embraced them with the fatherhood that the Son had revealed in the
fullness of time" (OA 3).

Jesus Christ is truly the center of God's loving plan. Hence with the epistle to   **3**
the Ephesians we reaffirm: "Praised be the God and Father of our Lord Jesus
Christ, who has bestowed on us in Christ every spiritual blessing in the
heavens! God chose us in him before the world began to be holy and blameless
in his sight, to be full of love; he likewise predestined us through Christ Jesus
to be his adopted sons . . . (Eph 1:3-5).

We celebrate Jesus Christ, who died for our sins and is risen for our
justification (see Rom 4:25), who lives among us and is our "hope of glory"
(Col 1:27). He is the image of the invisible God, the first-born of all creatures.
He sustains creation, and all human paths converge on him; he is the Lord of
ages. Beset by problems and crosses, we nevertheless intend to continue to
serve as witnesses on our continent to God's love and prophets of that
imperishable hope. We want to "inaugurate a new age under the sign of hope"
(OA V).

1. PROFESSION OF FAITH

4   We bless God who in his merciful love "sent forth his son born of a woman" (Gal 4:4) to save all people. Jesus Christ thus became one of us (cf. Heb 2:17). Anointed by the Holy Spirit (see Lk 1:15), in the fullness of time he proclaimed the good news, "This is the time of fulfillment. The reign of God is at hand! Reform your lives and believe in the gospel!" (Mk 1:15). This reign ushered in by Jesus first of all reveals God's self to us as "a loving Father full of compassion" (RM 13), who invites all, men and women, to enter it.

In order to emphasize this aspect, Jesus has drawn near particularly to those who were on the margins of society, and has proclaimed to them the "good news." At the outset of his ministry, he announces that he has been sent to "bring glad tidings to the poor" (Lk 4:18). To all who suffer rejection and contempt, who are aware of what they lack, Jesus says "Blessed are you who are poor" (Lk 6:20). Thus the needy and sinners can sense that God loves them, that they are the object of his enormous affection (cf. Lk 15:1-32).

5   Entry into the reign of God takes place through faith in the word of Jesus, which is sealed through baptism and witnessed by following him and sharing his life, death, and resurrection (cf. Rom 6:9). Entering God's reign thus demands a profound conversion (see Mk 1:15; Mt 4:17), a break with any kind of selfishness in a world marked by sin (see Mt 7:21; Jn 14:15; RM 13); in other words, embracing the proclamation of the Beatitudes (see Mt 5: 1-10).

The mystery of the reign, which has been hidden in God from ages and generations past (cf. Col 1: 26) and is now present in the life and words of Jesus and identified with his person, is the Father's gift (see Lk 12:32; Mt 20:23). It consists of the gratuitously offered communion of the human being with God (see EN 9; Jn 14:23), which begins in this life and reaches fulfillment in eternity (see EN 27).

God's love is attested in fraternal love (cf. 1 Jn 4: 20) from which it is inseparable: "Yet if we love one another God dwells in us, and his love is brought to perfection in us" (1 Jn 4:12). "The kingdom's nature . . . is one of communion among all human beings—with one another and with God" (RM 15).

6   In order to bring about the reign, Jesus "named twelve as his companions whom he would send to preach. . ." (Mk 3:14). To them he revealed the "mysteries" of the Father and made them his friends (cf. Jn 15:15). They were to continue the very mission that he had received from his Father (see Jn 20:21). He also made Peter the foundation of the new community (see Mt 16:18).

Before going to the Father, Jesus instituted the sacrament of his love, the eucharist (see Mk 14:22), the commemoration of his sacrifice. In this way, the Lord remains in the midst of his people to feed them with his body and blood, strengthening and expressing the communion and solidarity that ought to reign among Christians as they journey along earth's paths in the hope of fully encountering him. Spotless victim offered to God (see Heb 9:14), Jesus is likewise the priest who takes away sin through a single sacrifice (see Heb 10:14).

He and he alone is our salvation, our justice, our peace, and our reconciliation. In him we were reconciled to God and it is through him that the "ministry of reconciliation" (cf. 2 Cor 5:19) has been entrusted to us. He tears down any wall separating human beings and peoples (cf. Eph 2:14). Therefore today, in this period of new evangelization, we want to reiterate with the apostle Saint Paul: "Be reconciled to God!" (2 Cor 5:20).

We confess that Jesus, truly risen and ascended into heaven, is Lord,   7 consubstantial with the Father; in him "the fullness of deity resides in bodily form" (Col 2:9); seated at the Father's right hand, he is worthy of our adoration. "The resurrection gives a universal scope to Christ's message, his actions, and his whole mission" (RM 16). Christ rose in order to communicate his life to us. From his fullness we have all received grace (cf. Jn 1:16). Jesus Christ, who died to free us from sin and death, has risen to make us God's children in him. If he has not risen "our preaching is void of content and your faith is empty too" (1 Cor 15:14). He is our hope (cf. 1 Tm 1:1; 3:14-16), since he can save those who approach God, and is ever ready to intercede on our behalf (cf. Heb 7:25).

As Jesus had promised, the Holy Spirit was poured out over the apostles as they were gathered with Mary in the upper room (see Acts 1:12-14; 2:1). With the granting of the Spirit on Pentecost, the Church was sent to proclaim the gospel. Since that day, as God's new people (cf. 1 Pt 2:9-10) and body of Christ (cf. 1 Cor 12:27; Eph 4:12) it exists for the sake of the kingdom, of which it is seed, sign, and instrument (see RM 18) until the end of time. From that moment until the present, through preaching and baptism, the Church begets new children of God who are conceived by the Holy Spirit and born of God (see LG 64).

In the communion of the apostolic faith, which was confessed in Palestine   8 through Peter—"You are the Messiah, the Son of the living God" (Mt 16:16)—today we make our own the words of Paul VI, of which John Paul II reminded us as we initiated our labors: "Christ! Christ, our beginning. Christ, our life and our guide. Christ our hope and our end. . . . May no other light hover over this assembly than that of Christ, light of the world. May no other truth draw our minds, than the words of the Lord, our one Master. May we have no other aspiration than to be utterly faithful to him. May no other hope sustain us, than that which bolsters our weakness through his word. . . " (OA 1).

Yes, we confess that Jesus Christ is true God and true human being. He is the only Son of the Father, made human in the womb of the Virgin Mary, through the Holy Spirit, who came into the world to free us from all slavery to sin, to give us the grace of filial adoption, and to reconcile us to God and to other human beings. He is the living gospel of the Father's love. In him, humankind finds the measure of its dignity and the meaning and direction of its development.

9   We acknowledge the dramatic situation in which sin places the human being. For although the human being was created good, in God's own image, and is the lord who is responsible over creation, by sinning that same human being now stands at odds with God, is internally divided, has broken solidarity with neighbor, and has destroyed the harmony of nature. Thus we acknowledge the source of the individual and collective evils that grieve us in Latin America: wars, terrorism, drugs, dire poverty, oppression and injustice, institutionalized lying, the marginalization of ethnic groups, corruption, assaults on the family, abandoned children and old people, campaigns against life, abortion, the utilization of women, the pillaging of the environment—in a word, everything that typifies a culture of death.

Who will free us from these forces of death (cf. Rom 7:24)? Only the grace of our Lord Jesus Christ, offered once more to the men and women of Latin America, as a call to conversion of heart. The renewed evangelization that we are now undertaking must be an invitation to the conversion of personal and collective conscience alike (cf. OA 18) so that we Christians may be the soul, as it were, in all realms of society (cf. *Letter to Diognetus,* 8).

10   Identified with Christ living in each individual (cf. Gal 2:20), and led by the Holy Spirit, the children of God receive the law of love in their hearts. Thus they are enabled to respond to the demand that they be perfect like the Father in heaven (cf. Mt 5:48), following Jesus Christ and carrying their cross every day, even to the point of giving their lives for him (cf. Mk 8:34-36).

11   We believe in the one, holy, catholic, and apostolic Church, and we love it. It was established by Jesus Christ "on the foundation of the apostles" (Eph 2:20) whose successors, the bishops, preside over the various local Churches.

United in communion among themselves and presided over in charity by the bishop of Rome, they serve their local Churches and thus Christ's Church is alive and active in each of them. "The first beneficiary of salvation is the Church. Christ won the Church for himself at the price of his own blood and made the Church his co-worker in the salvation of the world" (RM 9).

The Church is present as a pilgrim on this continent, and it takes the form of a community of brothers and sisters under the guidance of the bishops. Gathered by the Holy Spirit (cf. CD 11) around the word of God and the eucharistic table, the faithful and pastors alike are sent to announce the gospel, by announcing Jesus Christ and offering the witness of fraternal love.

12 "The pilgrim Church is of its very nature missionary since it draws its origin from the mission of the Son and the mission of the Holy Spirit, in accordance with the plan of God the Father" (AG 2). Evangelization is its *raison d'être*; it exists in order to evangelize (cf. EN 15). The moment has come for Latin America, now providentially prompted by a new evangelical ardor, to carry its faith to those peoples that still do not know Christ, fully confident that "faith is strengthened when it is given to others" (OA 28).

Today, the Church intends to carry out a new evangelization that may transmit, strengthen, and make mature among our peoples their faith in God, Father of our Lord Jesus Christ. This evangelization must "always contain—as the foundation, center, and, at the same time, summit of its dynamism—a clear proclamation that, in Jesus Christ, the Son of God made man, who died and rose from the dead, salvation is offered to all men, as a gift of God's grace and mercy" (EN 27).

13 By its own inherent strength, the Christian proclamation tends to heal, strengthen, and advance human beings and to establish a fraternal community, by renewing humanity itself and endowing it with its full human dignity, through the newness of baptism and life according to the gospel (cf. EN 18). Evangelization promotes integral development, by demanding that all fully respect their rights and fully observe their duties so as to create a just and solidary society en route to its completion in the ultimate reign. The human being is called to collaborate with Jesus Christ and be his instrument in evangelization. In Latin America—a continent both religious and long-suffering—we urgently need a new evangelization, one that can announce forthrightly the gospel of justice, love, and mercy.

We know that through the incarnation Christ has been united in some fashion to every human being (cf. GS 22). He is the perfect revelation of the human being to the human being, and it is he who unveils the grandeur of the human vocation (cf. GS 22). Jesus Christ takes his place at the heart of humankind and invites all cultures to let themselves be drawn toward fulfillment by his spirit by elevating in them what is good and purifying what bears the mark of sin. All evangelization must therefore mean inculturating the gospel. Every culture can thus become Christian, that is, point toward Christ and draw inspiration from him and his message (cf. John Paul II, *Address to the Second Assembly of the Pontifical Commission for Latin America* [June 14, 1991], 4). Jesus Christ is indeed the standard for every culture and every human endeavor. The inculturation of the gospel is an imperative of following Jesus and it is necessary in order to restore the disfigured countenance of the world (cf. LG 8). This effort takes place within the striving and aspiration of each people, strengthening its identity and liberating it from the powers of death. Hence we can confidently proclaim: Men and women of Latin America, open your hearts to Jesus Christ! He is the way, the truth, and the life. One who follows him walks not in darkness! (cf. Jn 14:8; 8:12).

14   We believe that Christ the Lord is to return to bring God's reign to its fullness and hand it over to the Father (cf. 1 Cor 15:24), when all creation has been transformed into the "new heavens and a new earth where . . . the justice of God will reside" (2 Pt 3:13). There we will attain the perfect communion of heaven, enjoying the eternal vision of the Trinity. With sin, the devil, and death finally defeated, men and women who have remained faithful to the Lord will attain their full humanity as they share in the divine nature itself (cf. 2 Pt 1:4). Then Christ will recapitulate and fully reconcile creation; all will be his, and God will be all in all (cf. 1 Cor 15:28).

15   We want to confirm the faith of our people by proclaiming that the Virgin Mary, Mother of Christ and of the Church, is the first of the redeemed and the first believer. A woman of faith, Mary has been fully evangelized; she is the most perfect disciple and evangelizer (cf. Jn 2:1-12). In her testimony of prayer, of hearing the word of God, and of being ready to serve the reign faithfully, even to the cross, she is the model for all disciples and evangelizers. Her maternal figure played a decisive role in aiding the men and women of Latin America to acknowledge their own dignity as children of God. Mary is the distinguishing feature of our continent's culture. Mother and educator of the newborn Latin American people, Saint Mary of Guadalupe, through Blessed Juan Diego, "provides an example of a perfectly inculturated evangelization" (OA 24). She has preceded us in the pilgrimage of faith and on the road to glory, and she accompanies our peoples who lovingly call on her until we all finally come together with her Son. We joyfully and gratefully accept the magnificent gift of her motherhood and her tender protection, and we aspire to love her just as Jesus Christ loved her. We therefore invoke her as Star of the first—and of the new—evangelization.

2. FIVE HUNDRED YEAR ANNIVERSARY OF
THE FIRST EVANGELIZATION

"In the peoples of the Americas, "God has chosen for himself a new people **16** whom he has . . . made sharers in his Spirit. Through evangelization and faith in Christ, God has renewed his covenant with Latin America" (OA 3).

1492 marked an all-important point in this process of preaching the good news. For "what the Church is celebrating in this commemoration is not more or less debatable historical events, but something magnificent and permanent that cannot be underestimated: the coming of the faith, the proclamation and spread of the gospel message on this continent. Moreover it celebrates it in the deepest and most theological meaning of that term, namely as Jesus Christ, Lord of history and of the destinies of humankind is celebrated," (John Paul II, *Sunday Address* [January 5, 1991], 2).

God's creative, caring, and saving presence was already with these peoples. **17** The "seeds of the Word," present in the deep religious sense of pre-Colombian cultures, was awaiting the fruitful sprinkling of the Spirit. Along with other aspects that needed to be purified, these cultures at their core offered positive elements such as openness to God's action, the sense of gratitude for the fruits of the earth, the sacred character of human life and esteem for the family, the sense of solidarity and shared responsibility for work performed in common, the importance of worship, belief in a life beyond earth, and so many other values that enrich the Latin American soul (see John Paul II, *Message to Indigenous People* [October 13, 1992], 1). This natural religiosity predisposed the indigenous peoples of the Americas to receive the gospel more readily, even though some evangelizers were not always disposed to recognize those values.

Consequently, the encounter between Iberian Catholicism and the cultures of **18** the Americas gave rise to a special process of amalgamation (*mestizaje*). While that process had conflictive aspects, it highlights our continent's Catholic roots as well as its unique identity. That amalgamation process, which is also observable in many forms of popular religiosity and *mestizo* art, represents the joining of what is perennial in Christianity with what is specific to the Americas. From the very outset it has spread throughout our continent. History teaches us that "a valid, fruitful and admirable labor of evangelization took place, thereby opening the way to the truth about God and the human being in the Americas—so much so, indeed, that the evangelization itself became a kind of tribunal for holding accountable those [sometimes unscrupulous colonizers who were] responsible for such abuses" (OA 4).

19   Initially, it was members of religious orders who led the way in the work of evangelization. That work, however, under the inspiration of the Holy Spirit, was a combined effort by the whole people of God, bishops, men and women religious, and lay faithful. Among these latter we should also note that baptized indigenous themselves were involved, and that as time went on, they were joined by African American catechists.

Men and women of holy lives were the privileged instruments of that initial evangelization. The pastoral means they employed were tireless preaching of the word, the celebration of the sacraments, catechesis, devotion to Mary, the practice of the works of mercy, denouncing injustice, the defense of the poor, and a special concern for education and human development.

20   The great evangelizers defended the rights and dignity of the native people and rebuked "the outrages committed against the Indians in the time of the conquest" (*Message to Indigenous People,* 2). The bishops also exemplify the same stance of prophetic condemnation which is combined with the proclamation of the gospel in their councils and other meetings, in letters to the kings of Spain and Portugal, and in decrees on pastoral visitation.

Hence, "at the time of this five century anniversary how could the Church, which in its religious, priests, and bishops has always stood alongside the indigenous people, forget the enormous suffering inflicted on the populations of this continent during the period of conquest and colonization? We must recognize the full truth about the abuses committed, due to the lack of love in those people who were unable to recognize in the indigenous people their brothers and sisters and children of the same God and Father" (*Message to Indigenous People,* 2). Regrettably, this suffering has in some ways lasted until our own day.

One of the saddest episodes in the history of Latin America and the Caribbean was the forced transfer of an enormous number of Africans as slaves. Government and private bodies from almost all the countries of the Atlantic side of Europe and of the Americas were involved in the slave trade. The inhuman traffic in slaves, the lack of respect for life, for personal and family identity, and for ethnic groups are a scandalous disgrace in the history of humankind. With John Paul II we want to ask God's pardon for this "unknown holocaust" in which "baptized people who did not live their faith were involved" (*Homily on the Island of Gorée, Senegal,* February 21, 1992; *Message to African Americans,* Santo Domingo, October 12, 1992).

21   When we look at the more recent period of history, we continue to find the living traces of a centuries-old culture at whose core gospel is present. The lives of saints in the Americas attests especially to that presence. By fully living the gospel, they have been the most authentic, credible, and best qualified witnesses to Jesus Christ. The Church has proclaimed that many have possessed heroic virtue, from Blessed Juan Diego, an Indian, along with Saint Rose of Lima, and Saint Martin de Porres up to Saint Ezequiel Moreno.

On this five-hundred-year anniversary, we express gratitude to the countless anonymous missionaries, pastoral agents, and lay people, many of whom have worked in silence, and especially to those who have even given witness with their blood out of love for Jesus.

Part II

JESUS CHRIST EVANGELIZER LIVING IN HIS CHURCH

"Go, therefore, and make disciples of all the nations. Baptize them in the **22**
name of the Father, and of the Son, and of the Holy Spirit. Teach them to
carry out everything I have commanded you. And know that I am with you
always, until the end of the world!" (Mt 28:19-20). "These words can be said
to contain the solemn proclamation of evangelization" (OA 2).

The Holy Father has called us together to commit the Church in Latin
America and the Caribbean to a new evangelization and to "draw up now a
new evangelization strategy for the next several years, a comprehensive plan
for evangelization" (*Address to the Second Assembly of the Pontifical
Commission for Latin America* [June 14, 1991], 4). We want to present some
elements that will provide a basis for implementing these guidelines in the
local Churches on our continent.

The new evangelization, which is the "all encompassing element" or the
"central idea" that has shed light on our conference, will serve as the basis
for our understanding of the true dimension of human development, which
must respond to "the delicate and difficult situation of Latin America today"
(*Letter of Cardinal Gantin,* December 12, 1990). The new evangelization
will also be the basis for our consideration of the challenge of the dialogue
between the gospel and the various elements that make up our cultures in
order to purify and improve those cultures from within by means of the
teaching and example of Jesus so as to come to a Christian culture.

Chapter 1

NEW EVANGELIZATION

All evangelization begins with Christ's command to his apostles and their **23** successors; it develops further in the community of the baptized, within living communities sharing their faith; and it seeks to strengthen the life of filial adoption in Christ, whose primary expression is fraternal love.

After inquiring what we mean by new evangelization, we will better be able to understand that its starting point is in the Church, in the power of the Spirit, in an ongoing conversion process that seeks to witness to unity within the diversity of ministries and charisms, and that lives its missionary commitment with intensity. Only an evangelized Church can evangelize.

The tragic situations of injustice and suffering in Latin America, which have become even more acute since Puebla, demand responses that can be given only by a Church that is sign of reconciliation and that bears the life and hope that spring from the gospel.

What Is the New Evangelization? **24**

The starting point for the new evangelization is the assurance that Christ holds "unfathomable riches" (Eph 3:8) that no age or culture exhausts and to which we human beings can ever turn to be enriched (cf. OA 6). To speak of a new evangelization is to acknowledge that an old one or a first one has already taken place. It would be incorrect to speak of a new evangelization of tribes or peoples who never received the gospel. In Latin America, we can speak in this fashion because a first evangelization took place here five hundred years ago.

To speak of a new evangelization does not mean that the previous one was invalid, sterile, or short-lived. Rather, it means that today Christians face new challenges and new questions that urgently require a response. To speak of a new evangelization, as the pope noted in his opening address to this fourth general conference, does not mean proposing a new gospel different from the first. There is only one gospel, but it can shed new light on those new problems.

The expression "new evangelization" does not mean reevangelizing. In Latin America, the point is not to act as though there were no first evangelization but, rather, to start from the many rich values it has left in place and proceed to complement them by correcting previous shortcomings. The new evangelization has emerged in Latin America as a response to the problems plaguing a continent where a divorce between faith and life leads to situations of injustice, social inequality, and violence that cry out. It means taking up the magnificent endeavor of energizing Latin American Christianity.

For John Paul II, the new evangelization is something operational and dynamic. It is first and foremost a call to conversion (cf. OA 1) and to the hope that rests on God's promises. Its unshakable certainty derives from Christ's resurrection, which is the primary proclamation and the root of all evangelization, the foundation for all human advancement, and the principle of all genuine Christian culture (cf. OA 25). It is also a new realm of vitality, a new Pentecost (cf. OA 30-31) in which the acceptance of the Holy Spirit will give rise to a renewed people made up of free human beings conscious of their dignity (cf. OA 19) and able to forge a truly human history. It is the combination of means, activities, and attitudes that can put the gospel into active dialogue with modernity and with the postmodern, in order to challenge them and to be challenged by them. It is likewise the effort to inculturate the gospel into the present situation of our continent's cultures.

25   The agent of the new evangelization is the whole church community in accordance with its own nature: we bishops, in communion with the pope; our priests and deacons; men and women religious; and all of us men and women who constitute the people of God.

26   The aim of the new evangelization is to form people and communities whose faith is mature and to respond to the new situation we are facing as a result of the social and cultural changes of modernity. It must take into account urbanization, poverty, and marginalization. Our situation bears the marks of materialism, the culture of death, the invasion of the sects, and a variety of religious offers being made. This situation also brings with it new values,

yearning for solidarity and justice, religious searching, and the abandonment of all-encompassing ideologies. The addressees of the new evangelization also include the middle class, those groups, populations, and living and working environments that are impacted by science, technology, and the mass media.

It is the task of the new evangelization to arouse a personal acceptance of Jesus Christ and the Church on the part of the vast numbers of baptized men and women whose Christianity is devoid of vitality, who "have lost a living sense of the faith, or even no longer consider themselves members of the Church and live a life far removed from Christ and his gospel" (RM 33).

The content of the new evangelization is Jesus Christ, gospel of the Father, **27** who with deeds and words proclaimed that God is merciful to all his creatures; that God loves human beings with a limitless love and has willed to enter into human history through Jesus Christ, who died and rose for us in order to free us from sin and from all its consequences and to make us sharers in his divine nature (John Paul II, *Homily in Veracruz, Mexico*, May 7, 1990). Everything acquires meaning in Christ. He bursts the narrow horizon within which secularism encloses human beings and returns to them their truth and dignity as children of God; he does not allow any temporal reality—neither the state, nor the economy, nor technology—to become for human beings the ultimate reality to which they must submit. In the words of Paul VI, evangelizing means announcing "the name, the teaching, the life, the promises, the Kingdom and the mystery of Jesus of Nazareth, the Son of God" (EN 22).

The renewing power of this evangelization will be found in faithfulness to God's word; it will be welcomed in the church community; and its creative breath will be the Holy Spirit, who creates in unity and diversity, nourishes the wealth of charism and ministry, and projects out into the world through commitment to mission.

What form is this new evangelization to take? The pope has answered: It is **28** to be new in its ardor, in its methods, and in its expression.

New in its ardor. Jesus Christ calls us to renew our apostolic ardor. To that end, he sends his Spirit who today is igniting the heart of the Church. The apostolic ardor of the new evangelization springs from being radically conformed to Jesus Christ the first evangelizer. Thus the best evangelizer is the saint, the person of the Beatitudes (cf. RM 90-91). An evangelization that is new in its ardor means a solid faith, intense pastoral charity, and steadfast fidelity, which under the Spirit's action, generates a mystique, an enthusiasm that irrepressibly proclaims the gospel and that can awaken credibility so that the good news of salvation may be accepted.

29 *New in its methods.* Our situations require new approaches to evangelization. Witness and personal encounter, the presence of Christians in everything human, and confidence in the saving proclamation of Jesus *(kerygma)* and in the activity of the Holy Spirit are all essential.

Under the impulse of the creator Spirit, we must draw on imagination and creativity so that the gospel will reach everyone in a pedagogical and compelling way. Since we live in an image culture, we must boldly use the means made available to us by science and technology, while never placing all our trust in them.

Moreover, we must use those means that can make the gospel reach the core of both person and society, down to the very roots of the culture, and "not in a purely decorative way as it were by applying a thin veneer" (EN 20).

30 *New in its expression.* Jesus Christ urges us to proclaim the good news in a language that will bring the perennial gospel closer to the new cultural realities of today. New expressions must be sought within the inexhaustible riches of Christ so as to make it possible to evangelize those circles affected by urban culture and to inculturate the gospel in the new forms of the culture now taking shape. The new evangelization must be more inculturated into the ways of being and living of our cultures, while keeping in mind the particular features of different cultures, especially indigenous and African American cultures. (It is crucial that we learn to speak in tune with the mentality and culture of our hearers, and in accord with their forms of communication and contemporary means of expression.) The new evangelization will thus follow the thrust of the incarnation of the Word. New evangelization demands that the Church undergo a pastoral conversion. Such a conversion must be in keeping with the council. It affects everything and everybody: in personal and community awareness and practice and in relationships of equality and of authority. It does so with structures and dynamisms that can make the Church ever more clearly present as an effective sign, and as sacrament of universal salvation.

1.1 The Church Called to Holiness   31

Doctrinal Perspectives

During this fourth general conference, like Mary, we have been listening to the word in order to communicate it to our peoples. We have sensed that the Lord Jesus was repeating the call to a holy life (cf. Eph 1:4) on which our whole missionary activity is based.

The Church, as mystery of unity, finds its source in Jesus Christ. Only in him can it produce the fruits of holiness that God expects of it. Only by participating in his Spirit can it transmit the authentic word of God to human beings. Only holiness of life nourishes and guides true human development and Christian culture. Only with him and in him can it give God, almighty Father, honor and glory throughout all ages.

Call to Holiness

The Church is a holy community (cf. 1 Pt 2:9) first through the presence   32 within it of the Lamb who sanctifies through his spirit (cf. Rv 21:22ff.; 22:1-5; Eph 1:18; 1 Cor 3:16; 6;19; LG 4). Hence its members must strive day by day to live following Christ and in obedience to the Spirit, "so as to be holy and blameless in his sight . . . full of love" (Eph 1:4). The new men and women that Latin America and the Caribbean need are those who have heard with a good and upright heart (cf. Lk 8:15) the call to conversion (cf. Mk 1:15); those who have been reborn through the Holy Spirit in accordance with the perfect image of God (cf. Col 1:15; Rom 8:29); those who call God "Father" and express their love for him by acknowledging their brothers and sisters (*Puebla Conclusions*, 327); those who are blessed because they share in the joy of the kingdom of heaven; those who are free with the freedom that comes from truth and who stand in solidarity with all human beings, especially those who suffer the most. In the Blessed Virgin the Church has attained the perfection by which she has neither stain nor wrinkle. Holiness "is the key to the renewed ardor of the new evangelization" (John Paul II, *Homily in Salto, Uruguay* [May 9, 1988], 4).

Called Together by the Word

A holy community called together by the word, the Church has as one of its   33 primary duties to preach the gospel (cf. LG 25). We bishops of the local pilgrim Churches in Latin America and the Caribbean and all of us who are participating in this gathering in Santo Domingo want to assume with the renewed ardor required by our time the call issued by the pope, Peter's successor, to undertake a new evangelization. In doing so, we are quite conscious that evangelizing necessarily means proclaiming with joy the name, teaching, life, promises, reign, and mystery of Jesus of Nazareth, Son of God (cf. EN 22).

Kerygma and catechesis. Because many baptized Latin Americans have not personally accepted Jesus Christ through an initial conversion, the Church in its prophetic ministry must make it a basic priority to proclaim vigorously Jesus dead and risen (*kerygma*) (cf. RM 44), "the root of all evangelization, the foundation for all promotion of human development, and the principle of all genuine Christian culture" (OA 25)

This prophetic ministry of the Church also includes catechesis which, by continually making present God's loving revelation manifested in Jesus Christ, leads incipient faith to maturity and educates the true disciple of Jesus Christ (cf. CT 19). Faith should be nourished on God's word as read and interpreted in the Church and celebrated in the community so that pondering the mystery of Christ may help it to present that mystery as good news in the actual situations in which our peoples find themselves.

The service that theologians provide for the people of God likewise belongs to the prophetic ministry of the Church (cf. OA 7). Their task, which is rooted in God's word and carried out in open dialogue with the pastors and in complete fidelity to the magisterium, is noble and necessary. When carried out in this fashion their efforts can make a contribution to the inculturation of the faith and the evangelization of cultures. It may also serve to nourish a theology capable of energizing pastoral work and promote the whole of Christian life toward the pursuit of holiness. Theological effort thus understood stimulates work on behalf of social justice, human rights, and solidarity with the poorest.

Nevertheless, we are not forgetting that all of "God's holy people" share in Christ's prophetic function, and that it is exercised first by "spread[ing] abroad a living witness to Him, especially by means of a life of faith and charity" (LG 12). The witness of Christian life is the primary and irreplaceable form of evangelization, as Jesus forcefully demonstrated on a number of occasions (cf. Mt 7:21-23; 25:31-46; Lk 10:37; 19:1-10), and as the apostles also taught (cf. Jas 2:14-18).

Liturgical Celebration

The holy Church finds in the life of prayer, praise, and thanksgiving that **34** heaven and earth direct to God for his "mighty and wonderful" works (cf. Rv 15:3f; 7:9-17) the ultimate reason for its own convocation. That is why the liturgy "is the summit toward which the activity of the Church is directed; [and] at the same time . . . the fountain from which all her power flows" (SC 10). However, the liturgy is the activity of the whole Christ, Head and members, and as such, it must express the deepest meaning of his sacrifice to the Father: obeying by making its whole life the revelation of the Father's love for human beings. Thus, as the celebration of the Last Supper is essentially connected to Christ's life and sacrifice on the cross and makes it present every day for the salvation of all human beings, so also those who gather around the Lamb praising God are those who show in their lives the witnessing signs of Jesus' self-surrender (cf. Rv 7:13ff.). Hence Christian worship ought to express the twofold thrust of obedience to the Father (glorification) and of charity to brothers and sisters (redemption), for God's glory is that the human being live. Far from alienating people, therefore, worship frees them and makes them brothers and sisters.

When carried out in the Church in this fashion, liturgical service has in itself **35** an evangelizing power that ought to be made very prominent in the new evangelization. In the liturgy, Christ the Savior is made present today. The liturgy is proclamation and realization (cf. SC 6) of the saving deeds that we are enabled to touch sacramentally; hence, it convokes, celebrates, and commissions. The liturgy is an exercise of faith and is profitable for faith whether robust or weak, and even for the nonbeliever (cf. 1 Cor 14:24- 25). It sustains commitment to human development since it leads believers to accept their responsibility for building the reign in order to "make it plain that those who believe in Christ, though indeed they are not of this world, are nevertheless the light of the world" (SC 9). Liturgical celebration cannot be something separated from life or parallel to it (cf. 1 Pt 1:15). Finally, it is particularly through the liturgy that the gospel penetrates into the very heart of cultures. The entire liturgical ceremony of each sacrament also has a pedagogical value; the language of signs is the best way for Christ's message to "permeate people's awareness and [be] projected into the ethos of a people, its essential attitudes, its institutions and all its structures" (OA, 20; John Paul II, *Address to Intellectuals in Medellín* [July 5, 1986], 2). Hence the forms of liturgical celebration must be apt for expressing the mystery being celebrated and at the same time clear and intelligible to men and women (John Paul II, *Address to UNESCO* [June 2, 1980], 6).

Popular Religiosity

36   Popular religiosity is a privileged expression of the inculturation of faith. It involves not only religious expressions but also values, criteria, behaviors, and attitudes that spring from Catholic dogma and constitute the wisdom of our people, shaping their cultural matrix. This way of celebrating the faith, which is so important in the life of the Church in Latin America and the Caribbean, is present in our pastoral concern. Paul VI's words (see EN 48), which the Puebla Conference accepted and developed into clear proposals, are still valid today (cf. *Puebla Conclusions,* 444ff.). We must reaffirm our intention to continue our efforts to understand better and to accompany pastorally our peoples' ways of feeling and living, and of understanding and expressing the mystery of God and Christ, in order that, purified of their possible limitations and distortions, they may come to find their proper place in our local Churches and their pastoral activity.

Contemplation and Commitment

37   We want to conclude these words about the Church as mystery of communion, which is fully achieved in the holiness of its members, by calling to mind the contemplative and monastic life as it exists in Latin America today, and thanking God for it. Holiness, which is the unfolding of the life of faith, hope, and charity that received in baptism, seeks to contemplate the God of love and Jesus Christ his Son. Prophetic activity can be understood and is true and authentic only on the basis of a real and loving encounter with God who lures irresistibly (Am 3:8; Jer 20:7-9; Hos 2:16f.). When a capacity for contemplation is lacking, the liturgy, which is access to God through signs, becomes a shallow activity. We thank God for the presence of men and women dedicated to contemplation in a life based on the evangelical counsels. They are a living sign of the holiness of the whole people of God. They also constitute a powerful call to all Christians to grow in prayer which gives expression to ardent, committed faith; to faithful love contemplating God in the inner life of the Trinity and in God's saving action in history; and to unshakable hope in him who is to return to draw us into the glory of his Father who is likewise our Father (cf. Jn 20:17).

Pastoral Challenges

38   These observations on the holiness of the Church, its prophetic character, and its vocation to celebration lead us to recognize certain challenges that we regard as fundamental. They must be met in order that the Church in Latin America and the Caribbean may fully be the mystery of communion of human beings with God and with one another. Prayer groups, apostolic movements, new forms of life and of contemplative spirituality, as well as various expressions of popular religiosity are spreading within the Church. Many lay people are becoming aware of their pastoral responsibility in the various forms it takes. Interest in the Bible is growing, thus demanding a biblical pastoral activity adequate to offer the laity criteria for responding to the subtle accusations and appeals of a fundamentalist interpretation or to the tendency to withdraw from life in the Church and take refuge in sects.

39 Very often our own Catholics are unaware of the truth about Jesus Christ and of the fundamental truths of the faith; sometimes this ignorance goes along with a loss of the sense of sin. Popular religiosity, its wonderful positive features notwithstanding, has not been purified of elements foreign to genuine Christian faith nor does it always lead to personal acceptance of Christ risen from the dead.

40 We do little preaching about the Spirit, who is at work in our hearts and converts them, thus opening the way to holiness, the development of the virtues, and the strength to take up Christ's cross each day (cf. Mt 10:38; 16:24).

41 All of this obliges us to insist on the importance of the initial proclamation (*kerygma*) and on catechesis. We thank God for the efforts of so many catechists, male and female, who carry out their service in the Church with sacrifice, which is often sealed with their lives. As pastors, however, we must acknowledge that much remains to be done. Religious ignorance is still widespread; catechesis does not reach everyone, and it often reaches people superficially with contents missing or in a purely intellectual way that lacks the power to transform people's lives and their environments.

42 The practice of "spiritual direction" has largely disappeared. Besides being a condition for the maturing of priestly and religious vocations, it is utterly essential for preparing more committed lay people.

43 A great deal remains to be done in the liturgy in order to assimilate into our celebrations the liturgical renewal stimulated by Vatican II and to help the faithful to make the celebration of the eucharist express their personal and communal commitment to the Lord. We are not yet fully aware of the significance of the centrality of the liturgy as the source and culmination of the Church's life. Many people are losing the sense of the "day of the Lord" and of its inherent demand for the eucharist; there is still little participation of the Christian community; and we see some people attempting to make use of the liturgy with no regard for its true ecclesial sense. Serious and ongoing liturgical formation in keeping with the instructions and documents of the magisterium (cf. apostolic letter *Vicesimus Quintus Annus,* 4) has been neglected on all levels. The process of a sound inculturation of the liturgy is still being neglected, and consequently liturgical celebrations are still for many people a ritualistic and private matter that does not make them conscious of the transforming presence of Christ and of his Spirit, nor does it translate into a commitment in solidarity to transform the world.

44   Consequently, in many Catholics—ourselves or some of our pastoral agents sometimes included—faith and life are out of joint. Lack of doctrinal formation and a shallow life of faith make many Catholics an easy target for the secularism, hedonism, and consumerism invading modern culture—or in any case, it prevents them from evangelizing that culture.

Pastoral Directions

45   The new evangelization demands a renewed spirituality which, illuminated by the light of the faith that is being proclaimed, may encourage genuine human development through God's wisdom and be the leaven of a Christian culture. We think it is necessary to continue and to augment the doctrinal and spiritual formation of the faithful starting with the clergy, men and women religious, catechists, and pastoral agents, clearly emphasizing the primacy of God's grace which saves through Jesus Christ in the Church, through living charity and through the efficacy of the sacraments.

46   Jesus must be proclaimed in such a way that encountering him leads to the acknowledgment of sin in one's own life and to conversion, in a deep experience of the grace of the Spirit received in baptism and confirmation. Hence we must restore appreciation for the sacrament of penance, and its pastoral practice must extend into spiritual direction for those people who demonstrate that they are mature enough to benefit from it.

47   We must endeavor to have all members of God's people take on the contemplative dimension of their baptismal dedication and "learn to pray" by imitating the example of Jesus Christ (cf. Lk 11:1), so that prayer may always be made a part of the apostolic mission in the Christian community and in the world. To the many people who are Christians, and yet look to practices foreign to Christianity for answers to their yearnings for an interior life, we should be able to offer the Church's rich teaching and long experience.

Such an evangelization presenting Christ and his divine life in us must **48** demonstrate the utter need to make our behavior fit the model he offers us. The effectiveness of the new evangelization demands that the lives of Christians be consistent with their faith. The specific conditions in which contemporary people are living must be known so that the faith can be presented to them in a light-giving fashion. It also requires a clear preaching of Christian morality that encompasses personal and family as well as social behavior. The practice of small communities receiving good pastoral attention is a good means for learning to live the faith in close communion with life and with a missionary projection. Apostolic movements also make a very significant contribution in this area.

The new evangelization must emphasize a *kerygmatic* and missionary **49** catechesis. The vitality of the church community demands that there be more catechists and pastoral agents who have a solid knowledge of the Bible, enabling them to read it in the light of tradition and the Church's magisterium and, thus, shed light on their own personal situation and that of their community and society on the basis of God's word. They will be especially effective instruments for inculturating the gospel. Our catechesis must follow a continual path from infancy to maturity and should use the most fitting means for each age and situation. Catechisms are very important aids to catechesis; they are both the way to, and fruit of, a process of inculturating the faith. The *Catechism of the Catholic Church,* announced by John Paul II, will guide the preparation of our future catechisms.

The prophetic function of the Church—proclaiming Jesus Christ—must **50** always evidence the signs of true "courage" (*parrhesia:* cf. Acts 4:13; 1 Thes 2:2), completely free of any of this world's powers. The Church's social teaching, which is the basis for, and the stimulus to, the authentic preferential option for the poor, must form part of any preaching and any catechesis.

Our local Churches, which reach full expression in the liturgy, and above all **51** in the eucharist, ought to promote a serious and continuing liturgical formation for God's people at all levels, so that they may live the liturgy spiritually, consciously, and actively. This formation ought to take into account the living presence of Christ in the celebration, its paschal and festive value, the active role of the assembly, and its missionary thrust. There should be a special concern to develop and give serious formation to those whose responsibility it is to lead prayer and the celebration of the word when there is no priest. Finally, we think that Sunday, the liturgical seasons, and the celebration of the liturgy of the hours must be given all their meaning and their evangelizing power.

52   Community celebration ought to help integrate into Christ and his mystery the events of one's life; it should bring about a growth in fraternity and solidarity; it should be attractive to all.

53   We must develop a liturgy that, in complete fidelity to the spirit that Vatican II sought to recover in all its purity, may strive to adopt the forms, signs, and actions proper to the cultures of Latin America and the Caribbean, within the norms laid down by the Church. In this task, special emphasis must be given to appreciating popular piety, which finds expression especially in devotion to the Blessed Virgin, pilgrimages, and shrines, and in religious feast days illuminated by the word of God. If we pastors do not make major efforts to accompany the expressions of our popular religiosity by purifying them and opening them to new situations, secularism will make further inroads into our Latin American people and the inculturation of the gospel will be made more difficult.

1.2   Vital, Dynamic Church Communities

54   "That all may be one as you Father, are in me, and I in you; I pray that they may be one in us, that the world may believe that you sent me" (Jn 17:21). Such is Jesus Christ's prayer for his Church. He has prayed that the Church embody unity, according to the model of trinitarian unity (cf. GS 24). Thus did the first Christians in Jerusalem strive to live.

Conscious that the historic moment we are living demands that we "sketch the countenance of a living and dynamic Church growing in faith, becoming holier, loving, suffering, committing itself and awaiting its Lord" (OA 25), we want to turn to discover the risen Lord, who today lives in his Church, entrusts himself to it, sanctifies it (cf. Eph 5:25-26), and makes it a sign of union of all human beings among themselves and with God (cf. LG 1).

We want to reflect this "countenance" in our local Churches, parishes, and other Christian communities. We seek to impart an evangelizing drive to our Church, one that grows out of an experience of communion and participation that is already being felt in various kinds of communities on our continent.

1.2.1 The Local Church

Local Churches have as their mission to extend "the presence and evange- **55**
lizing activity of Christ" (*Puebla Conclusions*, 224) to the various communities since they are "formed in the likeness of the universal Church; in and
from these Churches there exists the one unique catholic Church" (LG 23).

The local Church is called to embody the driving force of communion and
mission. "Communion and mission are profoundly connected with each
other; they interpenetrate and mutually imply each other, to the point that
communion represents both the source and the fruit of mission. . . . It is
always the one and the same Spirit who calls together and unifies the Church
and sends her to preach the gospel to the ends of the earth" (CL 32).

The local Church is likewise "organic communion . . . characterized by a
diversity and a complementarity of vocations and states in life, of ministries,
of charisms and responsibilities" (CL 20).

"In the unity of the local Church, which springs from the eucharist, is found
the whole episcopal college with Peter's successor as its head, as something
that belongs to the very essence of the local Church. Parishes and Christian
communities are to flourish around the bishop and in perfect communion
with him like vigorous cells of diocesan life" (OA 25).

In keeping with its nature and its mission of gathering the people of God in
a place or region, the local Church has firsthand knowledge of the life,
culture, and problems of its members and is called to use all its energies
under the impulse of the Spirit to carry out the new evangelization, human
development, and the inculturation of the faith in that location (cf. RM 54).

As a rule, our dioceses do not have enough well-trained pastoral agents. **56**
Many do not yet have a genuine and clear pastoral planning process. We
must move further along the path of communion and participation, which is
often hindered by the lack of a sense of Church and of a genuine missionary
spirit.

Hence it is absolutely necessary that we: **57**

-   Increase the number of people working in the various fields of pastoral
    action and provide them with adequate training in accordance with the
    ecclesiology of Vatican II and subsequent official church teaching.

- Set in motion comprehensive, organic planning processes to encourage the involvement of all members of the people of God, of all communities, and all the various charisms, and to guide them toward the new evangelization, including mission "to the nations."

1.2.2 The Parish

58 The parish—community of communities and movements—gathers human anxieties and hopes and awakens and guides communion, participation, and mission. It is "not principally a structure, a territory, or a building but rather 'the family of God, a fellowship afire with a unifying spirit.' . . . The parish is founded on a theological reality, because it is a eucharistic community. . . . The parish is a community of faith and an organic community, that is, constituted by the ordained ministers and other Christians, in which the pastor—who represents the diocesan bishop—is the hierarchical bond with the entire particular Church" (CL 26).

If the parish is the Church present amidst people's homes, it thereby lives and works deeply within the fabric of human society and in close solidarity with its aspirations and problems.

The parish has the mission of evangelizing; celebrating the liturgy; promoting human development; and furthering the inculturation of the faith in families, in Christian base communities, apostolic groups, and movements, and in society through all of these. As organic and missionary communion, the parish is a network of communities.

59 The process of parish renewal in both pastoral agents and the participation of lay believers is still proceeding slowly.

The questions facing urban parishes urgently demand solutions so that they can respond to the challenges of the new evangelization. The normal operating principles of parish activity are out of phase with the pace of modern life.

60 Our work must take the following directions:

- Renew parishes through structures that make it possible to subdivide pastoral activity into small church communities in which the responsibility of lay believers can come to the fore.

- Upgrade the formation and participating of the laity by training them to embody the gospel in the specific situations where they live or engage in activity.

- In urban parishes, joint planning in homogenous areas should be emphasized so that styles of activity for the new evangelization can be set up.

- Renew their ability to display both a welcoming attitude and missionary drive toward those believers who remain afar, and multiply the physical presence of the parish by creating chapels and small communities.

1.2.3 Christian Base Communities

The Christian base community (= CBC) is a living cell of the parish which, **61** in turn, is understood as organic and missionary community. The CBC, which is ordinarily made up of a small number of families, is called to live as a community of faith, worship, and love; it must be led by lay people, men and women adequately trained within the community process itself; the leaders must be in communion with their parish and the bishop.

"Basic Christian communities ... must always be characterized by a decisive universal and missionary thrust that instills in them a renewed apostolic dynamism" (OA 25). "These communities are a sign of vitality within the Church, an instrument of formation and evangelization, and a solid starting point for a new society based on a 'civilization of love'" (RM 51).

When they lack a clear ecclesiological foundation and are not sincerely **62** seeking communion, such communities cease being ecclesial and may fall victim to ideological or political manipulation.

We see a need to: **63**

- Reaffirm the validity of basic Christian communities by developing in them a spirit of mission and solidarity and seeking to integrate them into the parish, the diocese, and the universal Church, in keeping with the teachings of *Evangelii Nuntiandi* (58).

- Develop plans for pastoral activity to strengthen the training of the lay leaders who serve these communities in close communion with the pastor and the bishop.

1.2.4 The Christian Family

64   The Christian family is a "domestic church," the primary evangelizing community. "Despite the problems now besieging marriage and the institution of the family, it can still serve as the first and vital cell of society; it can create great energies that are necessary for the good of humankind" (OA 18). Pastoral work with families must be made a priority and, indeed, a basic, felt, real, and operative priority: *basic*, insofar as such work is on the frontlines of the new evangelization; *felt*, that is, a priority that the whole diocesan community accepts and assumes; *real*, insofar as the bishop and his parish priests will stand by it in a concrete and firm way; *operative* in the sense that it ought to be incorporated into joint-planned pastoral activity. Such pastoral activity must be up-to-date in its use of pastoral and scientific tools. Religious communities and movements in general must accept family pastoral work from within their own charisms.

1.3 In the Unity of the Spirit, with a Variety of Ministries and Charisms

65   Baptism makes us God's people and living members of the Church. Through the action of the Holy Spirit, we share in all the wealth of grace that the Risen One bestows on us.

It is this same Spirit who enables us to recognize Jesus as Lord and leads us to build up the unity of the Church from the various charisms that he entrusts to us for "the common good" (1 Cor 12:3-11). This is our nobility and our responsibility: to be bearers of the saving message to others.

66   Thus, Christ's salvific ministry (cf. Mt 20:28; Jn 10:10) is made present through the service of each one of us. We exist and serve in a Church with a wealth of ministries.

1.3.1 Ordained Ministries

67   The ministry of bishops in communion with Peter's successor, together with that of priests and deacons, is essential in order that the Church respond to God's saving design with the proclamation of the word, celebration of the sacraments, and pastoral leadership. The ordained ministry is always a service to humankind for the sake of the reign. We have received "the power of the Holy Spirit" (Acts 1:8) in order to be witnesses to Christ and instruments of new life.

Today, we turn to listen to the voice of the Lord, who is calling and sending us the challenges of the present moment. We want to remain faithful to the Lord and to the men and women to whose service we have been dedicated, especially to the poorest.

a) The Challenge of Unity

The council reminded us that our ministry has a community dimension: **68** episcopal collegiality, priestly communion, and unity among deacons. We already have bodies for coordination at the continental level and in each one of our local Churches. The effort to achieve unity with those religious who share in our pastoral work in every diocese is impressive. Nevertheless, we recognize that there are reasons for concern in our local Churches: divisions and conflict that do not always reflect the unity desired by the Lord. Furthermore, due to the shortage of ministers and the overload of work that some people have to bear in exercising their ministry, many remain isolated.

Hence we have to embody reconciliation in the Church, and we must travel further along the road of unity and communion among ourselves as pastors and with the persons and communities that have been entrusted to us.

We therefore propose: **69**

- To maintain those structures that exist to enhance communion between ordained ministers, devoting particular attention to the various subsidiary functions and without impugning lines of authority as established in church law. Such structures can be reexamined and reshaped as the need arises and in keeping with the lessons of experience to make their scope and nature more clear. Such arrangements include bishops conferences, ecclesiastical provinces and regions, priests councils, and, on a continent-wide level, CELAM.

- We especially want to encourage the spirit of unity and communion in the initial training of future pastors and the ongoing training of bishops, priests, and deacons.

b) The Need for a Deeper Spiritual Life

The priesthood proceeds from the depths of the inexpressible mystery of **70** God. Our priestly life springs from the love of the Father, the grace of Jesus Christ, and the sanctifying and unifying action of the Holy Spirit. That life is played out in service to a community so that all may become receptive to Christ's saving action (cf. Mt 20:28; PDV 12).

The 1990 Synod of Bishops and the post-synodal statement *Pastores Dabo Vobis* have clearly outlined the characteristic features of a priestly spirituality with deep insistence on pastoral charity (cf. PDV, ch. 3).

71   We therefore propose:

- To seek in our liturgical and private prayer and in our ministry an ongoing and deep spiritual renewal so that Jesus Christ may be ever present on our lips, in our hearts, and in the lives of each of us.

- To grow in the witness of holiness of life to which we are called with the aid of the means we already have at hand: "gatherings for priestly spirituality, such as spiritual exercises, days of retreat or spirituality" (PDV 80), and other means indicated in that post-synodal papal document.

c)   Pressing Need for Ongoing Formation

72   Saint Paul urges his disciple to revive the gift he has received through the laying on of hands (cf. 2 Tm 1:6). John Paul II has reminded us that the Church needs to present credible models through priests who are convinced and fervent ministers of the new evangelization (cf. PDV 8, and ch. 6).

There is a growing awareness of the inherent need for ongoing formation, understood and undertaken as a path of conversion and a means for remaining faithful. The concrete implications of such formation on the commitment of the priest to the new evangelization demand that specific channels be created and developed to assure that it take place. It is ever more obvious that the growth process must be accompanied, striving to make it possible to take on and respond to the challenges that secularism and injustice pose to that growth process. We should devote equal attention to priests who are old or sick.

73   We consider it important:

- To prepare proposals and programs for the ongoing formation of bishops, priests, and deacons; national clergy commissions; and priests councils.

- To encourage all ordained ministers to be in continual formation structured in accordance with the guidelines of the papal magisterium, and to support them as they do so.

d) Utter Need to Be Close to Our Communities

The good shepherd knows his sheep and they know him (cf. Jn 10:14). As **74** servants of communion we want to watch over our communities, generously surrendering ourselves and being models for the flock (cf. 1 Pt 5:1-5). We want our humble service to make all feel that we are making present Christ the head, the good shepherd, and the bridegroom of the Church (cf. PDV 10).

By being close to each individual person, pastors can share with them their situations of suffering and ignorance, of being poor and outcast, and their yearnings for justice and liberation. This is an entire program for living out more fully our role as ministers of reconciliation (cf. 2 Cor 5:18), by offering each individual reasons for hope (cf. 1 Pt 3:15) on the basis of Jesus Christ's saving proclamation (cf. Gal 5: 1).

- We bishops propose to better organize a ministry of accompanying our **75** priests and deacons in order to support those who are in especially difficult contexts.

- All of us ministers want to maintain a humble presence within our communities and to be close to them so that all may feel God's mercy. We want to be witnesses of solidarity with our brothers and sisters.

e) Concern for Permanent Deacons

The ministry of deacons is important for our service of communion to Latin **76** America. In a very privileged way, they are signs of the Lord Jesus, "who has come, not to be served by others, but to serve, to give his own life as a ransom for the many" (Mt 24:12).

Because he is both an ordained minister and very much a part of complex human situations, the permanent deacon has a broad field for service on our continent in a new evangelization that may respond to the needs of human development and gradually lead to a culture of solidarity by presenting the word and the Church's social teaching.

- We want to recognize our deacons more for what they are than for what **77** they do.

- We want to accompany our deacons in discernment so that they may obtain both initial and ongoing training appropriate for their situation.

- We will continue to reflect on the spirituality specific to deacons, which is based on Christ the servant, so that with a deep sense of faith they may live out their commitment to the Church and their incorporation into the diocesan body of priests.

- We want to aid married deacons so that they may be faithful to their twofold sacramentality—that of matrimony and of holy orders—and so that their wives and children many live and share the diaconate with them. Their experience of work and their role as parents and spouses makes them very well qualified co-workers for addressing the various situations demanding attention in our local Churches.

- We propose to create the space necessary so that deacons may help in developing the services that the Church provides, by detecting and developing leaders, and promoting the shared responsibility of all in working toward a culture of reconciliation and solidarity. The deacon is the only kind of ordained minister who can reach some situations and places, especially isolated rural areas and densely populated urban areas.

1.3.2   Vocations to the Priestly Ministry and Seminaries

78   "In those days he departed to the mountain to pray, and he spent the night in prayer to God. When day came, he called his disciples to himself, and from them he chose Twelve, whom he also named apostles . . ." (Lk 6:12-13; Mk 3:13-14).

"At the sight of the crowds, his heart was moved with pity for them because they were troubled and abandoned, like sheep without a shepherd" (Mt 9:36-38).

Within a Church of "communion for mission," the Lord who calls us all to holiness calls some to priestly service.

a)   Pastoral Work for Vocations: A Priority

79   The facts before us are undeniable: priestly vocations are on the rise, and there is a growing interest in pastoral activity aimed at clearly presenting to young people the possibility of a call from the Lord.

However, those young people who are called cannot isolate themselves from contemporary changes in the family as well as cultural economic and social changes. Family breakdown can hinder one from experiencing love in a way that helps prepare for lifelong generous self-surrender. A contagious "permissive" consumer society does not encourage a life of austerity and sacrifice. Thus, it can happen that vocational motivation may be undercut by nonevangelical urgings even without the candidate's intention.

Hence we think it is important to: **80**

- Build vocational pastoral work into the overall pastoral work of the diocese and closely relate it to pastoral activity with families and youth. There is an urgent need to prepare pastoral workers, to find resources for this field of pastoral work, and to support the commitment of lay people to the promotion of consecrated vocations.

- Base vocational pastoral work on prayer, frequenting the sacraments of the eucharist and penance, catechesis for confirmation, Marian devotion, accompaniment through spiritual direction, and a specific missionary commitment. These are the main means that will help young people in their discernment.

- Make efforts to encourage vocations to arise out of all the cultures present in our local Churches. The pope has invited us to devote attention to vocations from native peoples (cf. *Message to Indigenous Peoples*, 6; *Message to African Americans,* 5).

- There is still a place for minor seminaries and similar kinds of centers   **81** when properly adapted to present conditions for young people in their last years of high school, when a strong desire for choosing the priesthood begins to emerge. In some countries and under very adverse family conditions, such institutions are necessary if young people are to grow in their Christian experience and make a mature vocational option.

- Since there is a resurgence of vocations among adolescents, we have the   **82** task of furnishing them with adequate encouragement, discernment, and formation.

- In our vocational pastoral work, we will keep the words of the Holy Father very much in mind: "An indispensable condition for the new evangelization is that there be many qualified evangelizers available. Hence the promotion of priestly and religious vocations . . . must be a priority for bishops and a commitment for the whole people of God" (OA 26).

b) Seminaries

83   The fact that major seminaries are springing up on our continent and that the number of students in them is growing is a sign of joy and hope.

Efforts are generally made to establish a climate favorable to spiritual direction and to be up-to-date in training future priests, especially in preparing them for pastoral work.

Nevertheless, we are concerned about the difficulty of finding a training team adequate to the needs of each seminary. The quality of training suffers as a result.

Due to the environment from which they come, candidates are often marked by very secularized ways of life or come to the seminary with limitations in their human or intellectual formation or even in the foundations of their Christian faith.

84   In view of these situations we propose to:

-    Fully assume the guidelines of the post-synodal exhortation *Pastores Dabo Vobis* and on that basis reexamine our basic *Norms for Priestly Formation* in each country.

-    Select and train those who provide formation, by taking advantage of courses provided by CELAM and other institutions. Before a seminary is opened there must be assurance that a formation team will be available.

-    Examine the direction of the formation provided in each of our seminaries to assure that it fits the needs of the new evangelization, which in turn has consequences for human development and the inculturation of the gospel. While maintaining the standards of a serious overall formation, particular concern must be directed to the challenge represented by the priestly formation of those candidates who come from indigenous and African American cultures.

-    Strive for a comprehensive formation that from the seminary onward may pave the way for the priest's ongoing formation.

1.3.3　Religious Life

As a gift from the Holy Spirit to his Church, one that belongs to the Church's **85** inner life and its holiness (cf. LG 44; EN 69), religious life is expressed in the heroic witness of many women and men religious, who on the basis of their unique covenant with God make the gospel's power present in even the most difficult situations. By faithfully living out the evangelical counsels, they share in Christ's mission and mystery; they irradiate the values of the reign; they glorify God; they provide encouragement to the church community itself; and they challenge society (cf. Lk 4:14-21; 9:1-6). The evangelical counsels are deeply paschal, since they entail being identified with Christ in his death and resurrection (see John Paul II, *Los Caminos del Evangelio* [*The Paths of the Gospel*], 17).

Through its experience of giving witness, religious life "must always be evangelizing so that those in need of the light of faith may accept the word of salvation with joy; so that the poor and the most forgotten may feel the closeness of fraternal solidarity; so that the outcast and abandoned may experience Christ's love; so that those who have no voice may feel that they are heard; so that those treated unjustly may find protection and aid" (John Paul II, *Homily in the Cathedral in Santo Domingo* [October 10, 1992], 8). The Virgin Mary, who is so deeply a part of the Christian identity of our Latin American peoples (cf. *Puebla Conclusions,* 283), is the model of life for those who have taken vows and a firm support for their fidelity.

On the basis of Vatican II and motivated by Medellín and Puebla, religious have been striving for renewal. They have sought to "return to the sources" and to the original inspiration of their orders and congregations (cf. PC 2). The role played by major superiors is very important for religious life. While respecting the purpose and spirit of each order or congregation, they deal with common issues and assure that the proper cooperation with the shepherds of the Church takes place (cf. CIC 708).

Since it is God's special gift to his Church, religious life must be ecclesial, and it enriches local Churches. Latin America's religious are renewing their allegiance to the pope. There must be an effort at greater mutual awareness between the various forms of religious life and the local Churches, based on the provisions of *Mutuae Relaciones.*

Contemplative life is uniquely fruitful for evangelization and mission. Its **86** entire life gives witness to the primacy of God's absoluteness. We are happy to see that the number of vocations to this kind of life is on the rise and that it is being extended to other countries.

87   The experience of secular institutes is significant, and they are growing. Through their consecration, they seek to harmonize the authentic values of the contemporary world with the following of Jesus as lived from within a secular situation. They should therefore occupy an important place in the effort of new evangelization for the sake of human development and the inculturation of the gospel.

88   Societies of apostolic life also make a generous contribution to this task of evangelization, and they are called to continue with their specific features.

89   Another form of consecration is that of virgins dedicated to God by the bishop of the diocese; they are mystical spouses of Jesus Christ who devote themselves to serving the Church (cf. CIC 604.1).

90   The woman who has taken vows helps permeate with the gospel our process of comprehensive human development, and she imparts a drive to the Church's pastoral work. She is often in the more difficult mission sites and is especially sensitive to the cry of the poor. Hence she must be given greater responsibilities in the planning of pastoral and charitable activity.

91   "The work of evangelization in Latin America," says the pope, "has been largely the fruit of your missionary service. . . . In our own time as well, men and women religious represent a primary evangelizing and apostolic force on the Latin American continent" (*Los Caminos del Evangelio,* 2.3).

In his letter to Latin American religious (*Los Caminos del Evangelio,* June 29, 1990), the Holy Father poses the following challenges: to continue "in the very front lines of preaching, always testifying to the gospel of salvation" (24); "To evangelize on the basis of a deep experience of God" (25); "to keep alive the charisms of your founders" (26); to evangelize in close collaboration with bishops, priests, and lay people, providing an example of renewed communion (cf. 27); to be in the forefront of the evangelization of cultures (cf. 28); to respond to the need to evangelize beyond our own borders.

Pastoral Directions

92   This fourth conference lays down the following commitments and pastoral guidelines with regard to religious life:

-     Recognize religious life as a gift to our local Churches.

-     Encourage the calling to holiness in religious women and men, by appreciating that their very existence and witness impart value to their life. Hence we want to respect and promote fidelity to each founding charism as a contribution to the Church.

- Engage in dialogue in mixed commissions and other bodies foreseen in the Holy See's document *Mutuae Relationes* in order to deal with the various tensions and conflicts on the basis of ecclesial communion. It is our intention that knowledge of the theology of religious life be encouraged in our seminaries and that in religious houses of formation particular importance be given to the theology of the local Church presided over by the bishop, and also to becoming familiar with the specific spirituality of the diocesan priest.

- We want to encourage initiatives by major superiors on behalf of initial and ongoing formation and spiritual accompaniment of men and women religious so that they may be able to respond to the challenges of the new evangelization. We will try to foster a missionary spirit so as to awaken in religious a yearning to serve beyond our borders.

- Support and assume the specific way of being and the missionary presence of religious in the local Church, especially when their option for the poor places them in front-line positions that are more difficult or entail a more committed form of involvement.

- Strive to assure that men and women religious who are working **93** pastorally in a local Church always do so in complete communion with the bishop and the priests.

1.3.4   The Lay Faithful in the Church and in the World

The people of God is made up primarily of lay Christian believers. As **94** Church—as both agents and addressees of the good news of salvation—they are called by Christ to exercise an utterly necessary evangelizing task in the world, which is God's vineyard. The words of the Lord are addressed to them today: "Go into the whole world and proclaim the gospel to every creature" (Mk 16:15; cf. CL 33). By virtue of baptism, the faithful are inserted into Christ and are called to live out the threefold priestly, prophetic, and royal function. The pastors in their particular churches should continually encourage them in their vocation.

a) Lay People Today in Our Churches

95 One of the signs of the times that we observe today is a large number of lay people committed to the Church; they exercise a variety of ministries, services, and functions in Christian base communities and are active in church movements. They are ever more aware of their responsibility in the world and in mission "to the nations." Thus, a sense of evangelization is growing among lay Christians. Young people are evangelizing young people; the poor are evangelizing the poor. Committed lay people indicate that they feel a need for formation and spirituality.

96 Nevertheless, it is obvious that the bulk of those baptized have not yet become fully aware that they belong to the Church. They feel that they are Catholic, but they do not feel that they are Church. Few make Christian values part of their cultural identity, and hence they feel no need to be committed to the Church and to evangelization. Consequently, the realms of work, politics, the economy, science, art, literature, and the media are not guided by gospel principles. Thus, there is an inconsistency between the faith people claim to profess and their real commitment in life (cf. *Puebla Conclusions,* 783).

It is also obvious that lay people are not always sufficiently accompanied by their pastors as they discover and mature in their own vocation. Because a certain clerical mentality persists in many pastoral agents—clergy and even lay—(cf. *Puebla Conclusions,* 784), and many lay people devote themselves to tasks within the Church and do not have an adequate formation, they are unable to respond effectively to the challenges of society today.

b) The Challenges Facing Lay People

97 The pressing needs of the present moment in Latin America and the Caribbean demand:

That all lay people be active agents of the new evangelization, human development, and Christian culture. Further development of the laity must be an ongoing process free of any clericalism, and it must not be reduced to matters within the Church.

That baptized people who are not evangelized be the primary targets of new evangelization. Such will truly be the case only if lay people conscious of their baptism respond to Christ's call to become active agents of the new evangelization.

In the context of ecclesial communion, there is an urgent need to encourage lay people to strive for holiness and to exercise their mission.

c) *Main Pastoral Directions*

- Deepen the experience of the Church as communion which leads us to **98** shared responsibility for the Church's mission. Encourage the participation of lay people in pastoral councils on the various levels within the Church's structure. Avoid having lay people reduce their activity to the realm of internal church matters by urging them to move into social and cultural circles and, within those circles, to be a driving force for transforming society in the light of the gospel and the Church's social teaching.

- Encourage the formation of lay councils in full communion with their pastors and yet sufficiently independent, so that they may serve as places for coming together, dialogue, and service and thus help strengthen the unity, spirituality, and organization of the laity. Such lay councils are also places for formation and may be set up in each diocese in the Church in every country. They can include apostolic movements, as well as lay people who are committed to evangelization but are not members of apostolic groups.

- Encourage comprehensive, gradual, and ongoing training of lay people **99** through agencies that may serve to "train trainers." They may also schedule courses and set up diocesan and national training centers, while devoting special attention to the formation of the poor.

- As an immediate pastoral objective, we will strive as pastors to intensify formation for lay people who are prominent in the areas of education, politics, the media, culture, and labor. We will encourage a specific line of pastoral work aimed at each of these areas so that people in those areas will feel that they have the full support of their pastors. Among those included will be the military, whose task it is to be ever at the service of the freedom, democracy, and peace of their peoples (cf. GS 79).

- Bearing in mind that all Christians are called to holiness, the pastors are to endeavor to provide all the proper means for helping lay people to have a genuine experience of God. They will also encourage the publication of materials specifically on lay spirituality.

- Encourage lay people to be organized on all levels of the pastoral **100** structure, based on criteria of communion and participation and respecting "the freedom for lay people in the Church to form such groups" (CL 29-30).

d) Ministries Conferred on Lay People

101   The Puebla document gathered up our continent's experience of lay ministries and provided clear guidelines in order to encourage, in keeping with the charisms of each person and the needs of each community, "special creativity . . . to establish ministries or services that can be exercised by the laity to meet the needs of evangelization" (*Puebla Conclusions*, 833; cf. 804-805; 811-817). The 1987 Synod of Bishops and the apostolic exhortation *Christifideles Laici* have insisted that it is important to show that these ministries "find their foundation in the sacraments of baptism and confirmation" (CL 23).

In keeping with the Holy Father's guidelines, we want to continue to encourage such experiences. They offer broad scope for lay participation (cf. CL 21- 23) and meet the needs of many communities. Without this precious collaboration, those communities would be left without anyone to accompany them in catechesis and prayer, and to encourage them in their social and charitable commitments.

We believe that "new expressions and new methods" for our evangelizing mission are finding broad areas in which they can be embodied in the "ministries, offices, and roles" that some carefully chosen and trained lay people may exercise (cf. CL 23). One such appropriate form might be that a whole family be given the pastoral responsibility for guiding other families, and that it be properly trained for that role.

e) Church Movements and Associations

102   In response to situations of secularism, atheism, and religious indifference, and as a fruit of the aspiration and need for the religious (cf. CL 4), the Holy Spirit has prompted the rise of movements and associations of lay people that have already produced much fruit in our Churches.

These movements give priority to the word of God and praying together, and they are particularly attentive to the action of the Spirit. Sometimes the experience of a shared faith leads to a need for a Christian sharing in goods, which is a first step toward an economy of solidarity.

Associations for the apostolate are legitimate and necessary (cf. AA 18). In accordance with the council, "Catholic Action" occupies a special place because of its deep connection to the local Church (cf. AA 20; CL 31). Since there is a danger that some movements and associations may become closed in on themselves, it is crucially important to bear in mind the "criteria of ecclesiality" indicated in the post-synodal exhortation *Christifideles Laici* (cf. 30). Such movements must be accompanied in a more clearly defined process of inculturation. The formation of movements with more of a Latin American stamp should be encouraged. "The Church expects a great deal of all those lay people who, enthusiastically and with the efficacy of the gospel, are involved through the new apostolic movements. Those movements, which reflect the need for a greater presence of the faith in the life of society, must be coordinated by means of overall pastoral planning" (OA 27).

f) Lay People, a Pastoral Priority

Because it is so important that the laity be present in the task of the new **103** evangelization, which leads to human development and ultimately permeates the whole of the culture with the power of the Risen One, we can state that as a result of this fourth conference, one of the main lines of our pastoral work must be that of a Church in which lay Christian believers are the active agents. A mature, committed, well-organized laity always in formation is the sign of local Churches that have taken the commitment to new evangelization very seriously.

1.3.5 Women

In Christ, fullness of time, the equality and complementarity with which **104** man and woman were created (cf. Gn 1:27), become possible since "there is not male and female; for you are all one in Christ Jesus" (Gal 3:26-29). Jesus welcomed women; he restored their dignity to them, and after his resurrection he entrusted to them the mission of announcing him (cf. MD 16). "Born of a woman" (Gal 4:4), Christ gives us Mary, who goes before the Church, eminently and uniquely standing as the model of Virgin and Mother (cf. LG 63). She forges history through her free cooperation, which attains the greatest degree of sharing with Christ (cf. *Puebla Conclusions*, 293). Mary has played a very important role in the evangelization of Latin American women; she has also made them effective evangelizers, as wives, mothers, women religious, workers, farmers, and professional people. She continually inspires them with the courage to give their lives; to bend over to help those in pain; to resist and to give hope when life is most threatened; to find alternatives when paths are being blocked; and to do so as an active and free partner who energizes society.

Situation

105   In our age, society and the Church have become increasingly aware that woman and man are equal in dignity. Although this equality is acknowledged theoretically, it is often ignored in practice. The new evangelization should firmly and actively promote the enhancement of women's dignity. Hence, we must delve more deeply into women's role in the Church and in society.

-    Today various reductionistic claims about woman's nature and mission are being propagated: her specifically feminine dimension is denied; her dignity and rights are slighted; she is made an object of pleasure and has a secondary role in the life of society. In response we want to set forth the gospel teaching on woman's dignity and calling, emphasizing her role "as mother, defender of life, and educator of the home" (*Puebla Conclusions,* 846).

106   A greater solidarity between men and women is gaining ground today, both within the family and in the building of the world, but further advances must be made toward real equality and toward the discovery that both find fulfillment in reciprocity.

In the family, in church communities, and in the various organizations within a country, it is women who most communicate, sustain, and promote life, faith, and values. For centuries, they have been the "guardian angel of the Christian soul of the continent" (John Paul II, *Homily in Santo Domingo* [October 11, 1992], 9). Such acknowledgment clashes scandalously with the fact that women are frequently excluded, their dignity is imperiled, and they are often subject to violence. She who gives and defends life is denied a decent life. The Church feels called to take a stand for life and to defend it in women.

Pastoral Commitments

107   We regard the following lines of action as urgent:

-    Courageously denounce assaults against Latin American and Caribbean women, especially farming and indigenous women, migrants, and workers, including assaults against their dignity committed by the mass media. Promote comprehensive formation so that people will become truly conscious of the dignity men and women have in common.

Prophetically proclaim woman's true essence, drawing from the gospel the light and hope of what she is in fullness without reducing it to passing cultural fashions. Create spaces in which women may discover their true values, esteem them, and openly offer them to society and to the Church.

- Make priests and lay leaders more conscious so that they may accept and appreciate women in the church community and in society, not only for what they do but especially for what they are. Encourage a stance of critical analysis toward media messages with regard to the stereotypes they present about femininity. In the light of the gospel of Jesus carry out a discernment among the movements struggling for women from various perspectives so as to energize their positive aspects, shed light on what might seem confused, and criticize what is contrary to human dignity. When we read the Scriptures, forcefully proclaim what the gospel means for women and develop a reading of God's word that may uncover the features that woman's calling contributes to the plan of salvation. **108**

- In education, develop new languages and symbols that will not reduce anyone to the category of object but rather will restore the value of each individual as a person; in educational programs eliminate material that discriminates against women by debasing their dignity and identity. It is important to implement educational programs on love and sex from a Christian perspective and to try to find ways in which interpersonal relations between man and woman will be based on mutual respect and esteem, acknowledgement of differences, dialogue, and reciprocity. Women must be incorporated responsibly into the decision-making process in all areas in both family and society. It is important that we have female leadership and that the woman's presence in organizing and leading the new evangelization in Latin America and the Caribbean be promoted. We must encourage the development of a kind of pastoral work that may advance indigenous women socially, educationally, and politically. **109**

- Condemn whatever affects woman's dignity by attacking life, such as abortion, sterilization, birth-control programs, and violence in sexual relationships; foster the means for assuring a decent life for those women who are most vulnerable: domestic servants, migrants, peasant women, indigenous, African American women, poor and exploited working women; intensify and renew pastoral accompaniment of women in difficult situations: separated, divorced, single mothers, children and women forced into prostitution by hunger, deceit, and abandonment. **110**

1.3.6   Adolescents and Youth

111   Jesus has gone through the same life-stages as every human person: childhood, adolescence, youth, adulthood. He reveals himself as the way, the truth, and the life (cf. Jn 14:5). When he was born, he took on the condition of a poor child and was subject to his parents; he had scarcely been born when he was persecuted (cf. Mt 2:13). That very Jesus, revelation of the Father who wills life in abundance (cf. Jn 10:10), restores the life of his friend Lazarus (cf. Jn 22), of the young son of the widow of Naim (cf. Lk 7:7-17), and of Jairus's young daughter (cf. Mk 5:21-43). Today he continues to call young people in order to give their lives meaning.

The mission of Latin American adolescents and young people who are on their way toward the third Christian millennium is to prepare themselves to be the men and women of the future, responsible and active in social, cultural, and church structures. Thus prompted both by the Spirit of Christ and their own creative spark to join in the effort to devise original solutions, they may help bring about a kind of development that is ever more human and more Christian (John Paul II, *Homily in Higüey, Dominican Republic* [October 12, 1992], 4).

Situation

112   Many young people suffer the effects of poverty, and of rejection by society, of joblessness and underemployment, of an education that does not meet the needs of their lives; they suffer from drug traffic, guerrillas, gangs, prostitution, alcoholism, and sexual abuse; many are tranquilized by advertising and propaganda and are alienated by cultural imposition and by a concern for short-term results that has created new problems for adolescents and young people in their process of emotional maturing.

Yet we find that some adolescents and young people stand up to the prevailing consumerism and become sensitive to people's infirmities and to the pain of the poorest. They strive to take their place in society by rejecting corruption and creating genuinely democratic areas for participation. More and more are joining together in ecclesial groups, movements, and communities to pray and engage in a variety of missionary and apostolic activities. Adolescents and young people are brimming with vital questions. Their challenge is to have a comprehensive personal and community life-direction that can give meaning to their lives so that they may thereby achieve their potential. A further challenge is the need to accompany them along the way as they grow in their faith and their work in the Church, and in their concerns to bring about the needed change in society through organized pastoral activity.

Young Catholics organized into groups in the Latin American Church ask **113** their pastors to accompany them spiritually and to support them in their activities. What they most need in each country, however, are clear pastoral directions that may help establish comprehensive pastoral youth activity.

Pastoral Commitments

We propose to implement the following pastoral actions: **114**

- Reaffirm the "preferential option" for young people announced at Puebla not merely in feelings but practically. That should entail a concrete option for a comprehensive pastoral activity with young people, involving accompaniment and real support, along with mutual dialogue among young people, pastors, and communities. To truly make an option for young people requires greater personal and material resources on the part of parishes and dioceses. Such pastoral work with youth must always have a vocational dimension.

In order to make that option we propose that there be pastoral activity: **115**

- That meets the needs for emotional maturing and the need to accompany adolescents and young people throughout the process of human formation and the growth of faith. Special importance is to be given to the sacrament of confirmation so that its celebration will lead young people to apostolic commitment and to be evangelizers of other young people.

- That develops an ability to be aware of, and respond critically to, the impact that culture and society have on them and helps them become committed to the Church's pastoral work and to the changes needed in society.

- That energizes a spirituality of following Jesus, brings faith and life **116** together, and promotes justice and solidarity, and that fosters an overall thrust that can give hope and create a new culture of life.

- That takes on new ways of celebrating faith proper to youth culture and **117** fosters creativity and the pedagogy of signs, while always respecting the essential elements of the liturgy.

118 - That proclaims in commitments assumed and in everyday life that the God of life loves young people and desires that they have a different future in which they will not be frustrated and excluded and in which a full life may be available to everybody.

119 - That can open participatory areas for adolescents and young people in the Church itself. That the pedagogy used in the educational process be experiential, participatory, and transforming. That it foster active involvement through the methodology of see, judge, act, review, and celebrate. Such a process must integrate the growth of faith into the human growth process, taking into account various elements such as sports, celebration, music, and theater.

- Such pastoral activity should keep in mind and strengthen all those organic processes that are valid and that the Church has extensively analyzed since Puebla. It will take special care to give prominence to pastoral work with youth in those particular *milieux* where adolescents and young people live and act: peasants, indigenous people, African Americans, workers, students, residents in the poor outskirts of cities, the marginalized, the military, and young people in critical situations.

- Through its word and witness, the Church must primarily present Jesus Christ in an attractive and inspiring way to adolescents and young people so that he may be their way, truth, and life and thus respond to their yearnings for personal fulfillment and their need to find a meaning to life itself.

120 - In order to respond to the contemporary cultural situation, youth pastoral activity must present the gospel ideals forcefully and in a way that is attractive and accessible to young people in their lives. It should foster the creation and leadership of energetic and gospel-oriented groups and communities of young people. Such groups may serve to sustain the educational process of adolescents and young people and sensitize and commit them to respond to the challenges of human development, solidarity, and building the civilization of love.

1.4 To Proclaim the Reign to All Peoples

121 Christ reveals the Father to us and draws us into the mystery of the trinitarian life through the Spirit. Everything passes through Christ who becomes way, truth, and life. Through baptism we receive divine filiation; having all become children of God, we peoples of Latin America have all become brothers and sisters to one another.

We have been drawn into the mystery of trinitarian communion because Christ has become one with us by taking on the condition of a slave and everything that is part of our human condition—except sin—in order to transform it, give it life, and make it ever more human and divine. In this fashion, Christ now enters into the heart of our peoples and takes up and transforms those peoples.

When we are incorporated into him, he communicates his life of love to us, as the vine to the branches, by pouring out his Spirit, who enables us to forgive, to love God above all things, and to love all our brothers and sisters without regard for race, nation, or economic situation. Thus, Jesus Christ is the seed of a new reconciled humankind.

In Latin America many people live in poverty, which often reaches shocking **122** levels. Even in limit-situations, however, we are able to love one another, to live in unity despite our differences, and to provide the world with our radiant experience as brothers and sisters.

We joyfully testify that in Jesus Christ we have integral liberation for each **123** one of us and for our peoples: liberation from sin, death, and slavery, which consists of forgiveness and reconciliation.

Jesus calls us together in his Church, which is sacrament of evangelizing communion. There we are to live the unity of our Churches in charity and to communicate and proclaim this communion to the whole world through the word, the eucharist, and the other sacraments. The Church lives in order to evangelize; its life and vocation are realized when it becomes witness, when it prompts conversion and leads men and women to salvation (cf. EN 15). "Thus the Church began the great task of evangelization on the day when the apostles received the Holy Spirit" (OA 2).

Jesus Christ gives us life in order to communicate it to all. Our mission **124** demands that in union with our peoples we be open to receive this life in fullness in order to communicate it abundantly to the churches entrusted to us, and beyond our borders as well. We ask forgiveness for our frailties, and we implore the grace of the Lord so that we may be more effective in carrying out the mission that we have received. We invite everyone, renewed in the Spirit, to also proclaim Jesus Christ and become missionaries of life and of hope for all our brothers and sisters. The new evangelization must be able to awaken a new missionary fervor in a Church that is ever more rooted in the perennial strength and power of Pentecost (cf. EN 41).

1.4.1 Projecting the Mission "to the Nations"

125 Arising out of the Father's saving love, the mission of the Son with power of the Holy Spirit (cf. Lk 4:18), which is the very essence of the Church (cf. AG 2) and fundamental object of this fourth general conference, is our primary responsibility.

In his encyclical on mission, John Paul II has led us to discern three ways of carrying out this mission: pastoral care in situations where faith is alive, the new evangelization, and missionary activity "to the nations" [ad gentes] (cf. RM 33).

We are renewing this latter sense of mission fully aware that new evangelization is impossible without a projection toward the non-Christian world, for as the pope points out: "It is in commitment to the Church's universal mission that the new evangelization of Christian peoples will find inspiration and support" (RM 2).

We are pleased that we can say that, out of our poverty, people have responded to the challenge of the mission "to the nations" proposed at Puebla and have shared the wealth of our faith with which the Lord has blessed us. We nevertheless acknowledge that awareness of mission to the nations is still insufficient or weak. Latin American Missionary Congresses (COMLAS), national missionary congresses, missionary groups and movements, and aid received from sister churches have served to motivate us to become aware of this gospel demand.

Pastoral Challenges

126 - There has not been enough insistence that we must be better evangelizers.

- We become enclosed in our own local problems and forget our apostolic commitment to the non-Christian world.

- We pass our missionary commitment on to some of our brothers and sisters to discharge for us.

The root of all this is the lack of an explicit program of missionary formation **127** in most seminaries and houses of formation.

We invite each local Church in Latin America to: **128**

- Bring the energy of mission into its ordinary pastoral activity, with the support of a diocesan mission run by a missionary team and moved by a living spirituality toward a creative and generous missionary action.

- Establish a positive relationship with the missionary activities of the papacy which should be put in the hands of a capable person and have the backing of the local Church.

- Encourage all of God's people to provide missionary cooperation, translated into prayer, sacrifice, witness of Christian life, and financial support.

- Incorporate into programs of priestly and religious formation specific courses in missiology, and instruct candidates for the priesthood on how important it is that the gospel be inculturated.

- Train native pastoral agents with a missionary spirit along the lines indicated in the encyclical, *Redemptoris Missio.*

- Courageously agree to send missionaries—whether priests, religious, or lay people. Coordinate human and material resources in order to strengthen the processes of training, sending, accompaniment, and reincorporation of missionaries.

1.4.2   *Reinvigorating the Faith of Those Baptized Who Are Afar*

Our God is a Father rich in mercy. God respects the freedom of his sons and **129** daughters and awaits the moment of return, going forth to meet those who have strayed far from their home (cf. Lk 15).

Pastoral Challenges

Many baptized people in Latin America and the Caribbean do not steer their **130** lives by the gospel. Many draw away from the Church and do not identify with it. These include many young people and those who are more critical of what the Church does, although they are not the only ones. Other people become uprooted from their religious environment when they move away from their native region.

Pastoral Guidelines

131 As pastors of the Church, we are concerned about this situation. We are likewise pained to observe that many of our faithful are unable to communicate to others the joy of their faith. Jesus Christ asks us to be the "salt of the earth," and leaven in the dough. Hence, while not neglecting to care for those who are near, the Church—both pastors and faithful—must go out to meet those who are far away.

The doors of many of these distant brothers and sisters are waiting for the Lord to knock (cf. Rv 3:20) through Christians who take on their baptism and confirmation in a missionary spirit and go out to meet those who have wandered far from the Father's house. Hence, we make these suggestions:

- Develop a new missionary drive toward these believers and go out to meet them. The Church must not remain content with those who accept and follow it more easily.

- Preach the *kerygma* to them in a lively and joyful manner.

- Organize missionary campaigns that can unveil the ever contemporary newness of Jesus Christ, especially through house visits and popular missions.

- Take advantage of those moments in which the baptized have contact with the Church, such as the baptism of their children, first communion, confirmation, illness, marriage, and funerals, in order to unveil to them the ever contemporary newness of Jesus Christ.

- Strive to approach through the media those who cannot be reached directly.

- Motivate and encourage ecclesial communities and movements to redouble their evangelizing service within the pastoral direction taken by the local Church.

1.4.3   Uniting All Brothers and Sisters in Christ

"That they may all be one, as you, Father, are in me and I in you, that they   **132**
may also be in us, that the world may believe that you have sent me" (Jn
17:21). This prayer of Christ is the basis for Vatican II's deploring of the
scandal of divisions among Christians (cf. UR 1), and it demands that we
find the most effective ways to attain unity in truth.

Pastoral Challenge

The great challenge before us is this division between Christians, a division   **133**
that for various reasons has been aggravated over the course of history.

- Confusion over the issue as the result of a deficient religious formation,
  among other reasons.

- Proselytizing fundamentalism by sectarian Christian groups who hinder
  the sound ecumenical path.

- We may regard the whole Jewish people as being in a situation similar   **134**
  to that of separated Christians. Dialogue with them is also a challenge
  to our Church.

Pastoral Guidelines

We therefore join John Paul II in saying: "Ecumenism is a priority for the   **135**
Church's pastoral activity in our age." In order to respond adequately to this
challenge we make these suggestions:

- Consolidate ecumenical work and spirit in truth, justice, and charity.

- Deepen relationships of convergence and dialogue with those Churches
  who pray the creed of Nicea-Constantinople, who share the same
  sacraments and who revere Holy Mary, Mother of God, even if they do
  not acknowledge the primacy of the Roman pontiff.

- Intensify ecumenical theological dialogue.

- Encourage prayer in common for Christian unity and especially the
  week of prayer for the unity of believers.

- Promote ecumenical formation in training courses for pastoral agents, especially in seminaries.

- Encourage study of the Bible between theologians and scholars in the Church and in Christian denominations.

- Maintain and strengthen programs and initiatives in the way of joint cooperation in the social realm and in promoting shared values.

- Appreciate CELAM's division for ecumenism (SECUM) and collaborate with its endeavors.

1.4.4   Engaging in Dialogue with Non-Christian Religions

136   "God, in an age-long dialogue, has offered and continues to offer salvation to humankind. In faithfulness to the divine initiative, the Church too must enter into a dialogue of salvation with all men and women" (DP 38). The Church is well aware that the dialogue it promotes has a witnessing character while at the same time the person and nature of the dialogue partner is to be respected (cf. *Puebla Conclusions,* 1114).

Pastoral Challenges

137   - The importance of deepening a dialogue with the non-Christian religions on our continent, and especially with indigenous and African American religions, which have been ignored or shunted aside for a long time.

- The existence of prejudice and misunderstanding as an obstacle to dialogue.

Pastoral Directions

138   In order to intensify interreligious dialogue, we think it is important to:

- Foster a change of attitude on our own part, leaving aside historical prejudices in order to establish a climate of trust and familiarity.

- Promote dialogue with Jews and Muslims despite the problems that the Church suffers in countries where these are the majority religions.

- Deepen knowledge of Judaism and Islam among pastoral agents.

- Encourage pastoral agents to develop a knowledge of other religions and manifestations of religion existing on our continent.

- Seek activities on behalf of peace, the promotion and defense of human dignity, and cooperation in defending creation and ecological balance as a way of coming together with other religions.

- Seek occasions for dialogue with African American and indigenous religions while being alert to discover in them the "seeds of the Word" with true Christian discernment, offering them the complete proclamation of the gospel and avoiding any kind of religious syncretism.

1.4.5   Fundamentalist Sects

The problem of the sects has reached dramatic proportions and has become truly worrisome, particularly due to increasing proselytism.   **139**

Fundamentalist sects are religious groups that insist that only faith in Jesus   **140**
Christ saves, that the only basis for faith is Scripture interpreted personally in a fundamentalist manner, and hence excluding the Church; they emphasize the end of the world and the proximity of judgment.

They are characterized by their very enthusiastic proselytizing through persistent house visiting and large-scale distribution of Bibles, magazines, and books; their presence and the opportunistic help they provide at times of personal or family crisis; and their great technical skill in using the media. They have at their disposal immense funding from other countries and the tithes they oblige all their members to pay.

Other features are a rigorous moralism, prayer meetings with a participatory and emotional Bible-based worship, and their aggressive stance toward the Church; they often resort to defamation and to material inducements. Although they are only weakly committed to the temporal realm, they tend to become involved in politics with a view to taking power.

Such fundamentalist sects have grown enormously in Latin America since the time of Puebla.

Pastoral Challenges

141   Provide an effective pastoral response to the advance of the sects by making the Church's evangelizing activity more present in the vulnerable sectors such as migrants, those populations unattended by priests or in which there is a great deal of religious ignorance, and simple people or those with material needs and family problems.

Pastoral Directions

142   -   Strive to make the Church ever more communitarian and participatory through ecclesial communities, family groups, Bible circles, and ecclesial movements and associations so that the parish becomes a community of communities.

-    Bring Catholics to personal acceptance of Christ and to the Church by proclaiming the risen Lord.

-    Develop a catechesis that can properly instruct the people by explaining the mystery of the Church, which is sacrament of salvation and communion, the mediation of the Virgin Mary and the saints, and the mission of the hierarchy.

-    Foster a ministerial Church by increasing the number of ordained ministers and encouraging properly trained lay ministers so as to enhance evangelizing service throughout God's people.

143   -   Reaffirm the Church's identity by cultivating its characteristic features such as:

a)   Devotion to the mystery of the eucharist, sacrifice and paschal banquet;

b)   Devotion to the Blessed Virgin Mary, mother of Christ and mother of the Church;

c)   Communion and obedience to the Roman pontiff and to one's own bishop;

d)   Devotion to God's word as read in the Church.

144   -   Strive to make the contemplative dimension and holiness a priority in all pastoral planning, so that the Church may bring about God's presence in contemporary human beings who so long for him.

- Create the conditions so that all ministers of God's people may offer a   **145**
  witness of life and charity, spirit of service, and a welcoming spirit,
  especially at moments of suffering and crisis.

- Promote a lively and participatory liturgy projecting outward toward
  life.

- Calmly and objectively provide the people with ample instruction on the   **146**
  features and differences of the various sects and on how to answer unjust
  accusations against the Church.

- Promote home visiting by trained lay people and organize a specific
  form of pastoral work aimed at welcoming Catholics back to the Church.

1.4.6   New Religious Movements or Free Religious Movements

In phenomenological terms, these are social and cultural groups whose drive   **147**
comes from poor segments of society but also from the middle and upper
classes in Latin America, who find a way of expressing their identity and
human yearnings in syncretistic religious forms. From the standpoint of
Catholic faith, these phenomena can be regarded as signs of the times and
as a warning that the Church is absent from some circles and must reexamine
its evangelizing activity.

Several currents or kinds of phenomena can be distinguished:

- Para-Christian or semi-Christian forms, such as the Jehovah's Witnesses and Mormons. Each of these movements has its own characteristics, but they share a proselytizing approach, millenarianism, and an
  organizational style similar to those of businesses.

- Esoteric forms that seek special enlightenment and share secret items of
  knowledge and a religious concern for the occult. Such is the case of
  spiritist, Rosacrucian, gnostic, theosophical, and similar currents.

- Philosophies and kinds of worship that have some oriental aspects but
  are rapidly adapting to our continent, such as Hare Krishna, Divine
  Light, Ananda Marga, and others, which offer mysticism and a communal experience.

- Groups that spring from the great Asian religions whether Buddhism (e.g., Seicho no Ié), Hinduism (e.g., yoga), or Islam (e.g., Baha'i), which are not only a manifestation of immigrants from Asia but are also taking root in some sectors of our society.

- Socio-religious enterprises, like the Moon sect or the New Acropolis, which have clear ideological and political aims along with their religious expressions in media crusades and proselytizing campaigns. They draw on help or inspiration from First World; with regard to religion they emphasize immediate conversion and healing, thus giving rise to the so-called electric Churches.

- A vast array of centers for "divine healing" or which deal with the spiritual or physical ills of people who have problems or are poor. These therapeutic cults serve their clients individually.

148   Since there are so many of these new religious movements and they differ a great deal from one to another, we want to center our attention on the reasons for their growth (cf. *Puebla Conclusions,* 1122) and the pastoral challenges they pose.

149   The explanations offered for why they arouse interest in some people are numerous and varied. Among them we should note:

- The ongoing and deepening social crisis, which arouses a certain collective anxiety and loss of identity and causes people to lose their roots.

- The ability these movements have to adapt to social circumstances and momentarily satisfy some needs of people. A taste for novelty certainly plays a role.

- The fact that the Church has become distant from some groups—whether poor or rich—who are seeking new channels of religious expression, but who also may be evading the commitments entailed in faith.

- Their ability to provide an apparent solution to the desires for "healing" on the part of people who are suffering.

Pastoral Challenges

150   - Our greatest challenge is to evaluate the Church's evangelizing activity

and to determine which circles it reaches and which it does not reach.

- Learn how to respond adequately to the questions people ask themselves on the meaning of life, on the meaning of our relationship with God, in the midst of our ongoing and deepening social crisis.

- Acquire greater knowledge of the identities and cultures of our peoples.

Pastoral Directions

In the face of these challenges, we propose the following pastoral directions: **151**

- Offer help for discerning life's problems in the light of faith. In this respect, we must restore the value of the sacrament of penance and spiritual direction.

- Strive to adapt our evangelization and celebrations of faith to the cultures and subjective needs of the faithful without falsifying the gospel.

- Engage in a deep reexamination of our pastoral work in order to improve the quality of the means we use and the witness we give.

- Treat religious movements in a differentiated way in accordance with their nature and their attitudes toward the Church.

- Foster a living liturgy in which the faithful may be drawn into the **152** mystery.

- Present a Christian anthropology, which provides the meaning of human potential, the meaning of resurrection, and the meaning of our relationships with the universe (horoscopes). Keep in mind that indifferentism must be combatted by adequately presenting the ultimate meaning of the human being. For that purpose a presentation of the last things will be very helpful.

1.4.7   Inviting the Godless and the Indifferent

The phenomenon of unbelief is growing in Latin America and the Caribbean **153** today. It is of concern to the Church, especially with regard to those who live as though they were not baptized (cf. EN 56).

One of its forms is *secularism,* which denies God, either because it holds that all things can be explained in themselves without any need to invoke God, or because it regards God as inimical and as alienating to human beings. This secularist position should be distinguished from the process known as *secularization,* which rightfully maintains that the material realities of nature and human beings are inherently "good," that their laws must be respected, and that freedom is for the sake of human self-fulfillment and is respected by God (cf. GS 36).

The other form is the *indifferentism* of those who either reject any religion because they regard it as useless or harmful for human life and hence are uninterested in it, or because they hold that all religions are equal and therefore none can claim to be the one true religion.

Pastoral Challenges

154 - *Secularism* is a serious challenge to the new evangelization since it regards God as incompatible with human freedom (cf. OA 11) and religion as a dehumanizing and alienating stance because it separates human beings from their earthly responsibility. Moreover, by rejecting dependence on the Creator, it leads to the idolatries of possession, power, and pleasure and to a loss of life's meaning by reducing human beings to their merely material value.

- *Indifferentism* also challenges the new evangelization because it cuts off the creature's relationship to God at the root, that is, it rejects any concern for religion and hence for the commitment of faith, or because it brings the figure of Christ down to where he is simply a teacher of morality or the founder of a religion alongside others of equal stature, thus denying that he is the sole, universal, and definitive savior of human beings.

- Likewise, both *indifferentism* and *secularism* undermine morality because they deprive human behavior of any ethical foundation and hence easily fall into the relativism and permissiveness that characterize contemporary society.

155 Many pseudo-religious movements of an orientalist cast and those of the occult, divination, or spiritism undermine faith and confuse people by providing false solutions to the great questions about human beings, that is, their destiny, their freedom, and the meaning of life.

Pastoral Guidelines

The new evangelization demands that we: **156**

- Provide formation in a faith that becomes life, initiating that faith by proclaiming the *kerygma* to those who are in the dechristianized world (cf. EN 51 and 52) and fostering it with the joyful witness of genuine faith communities in which our lay people live out the meaning of the sacraments.

- Cultivate a solid moral conscience so that in the complex circumstances of modern life our faithful may be able to interpret soundly the voice of God in moral matters and develop a gospel sense of sin.

- Educate Christians to see God in their own person, in nature, in all of history, in work, in culture, in the whole secular realm by discovering the harmony that according to God's plan should exist between the order of creation and that of redemption.

- Develop a way of celebrating the liturgy that may integrate the life of human beings into a deep and respectful experience of the unfathomable divine mystery of inexpressible wealth.

- Encourage pastoral activity suitable for the evangelization of university circles, where those who will play a decisive role in shaping culture are now being trained.

Chapter 2

HUMAN DEVELOPMENT

157 "Between evangelization and human advancement—development and liberation—there are in fact profound links. These include links of an anthropological order, because the person who is to be evangelized is not an abstract being but is subject to social and economic questions. They also include links in the theological order, since one cannot dissociate the plan of creation from the plan of redemption. The latter plan touches the very concrete situation of injustice to be combatted and of justice to be restored. They include links of the eminently evangelical order, which is that of charity: How in fact can one proclaim the new commandment without promoting in justice and in peace true, authentic human development?" (EN 31).

The ultimate meaning of the Church's commitment to human development, continually reiterated in its social teaching, lies in the firm conviction that ". . . genuine exterior social union has its origin in the union of minds and hearts, . . . in faith and love" (GS 42). "Through the gospel message, the Church offers a force for liberation which promotes development precisely because it leads to conversion of heart and of ways of thinking, fosters the recognition of each person's dignity, encourages solidarity, commitment, and service of one's neighbor" (RM 59). "In carrying on these activities, however, she never loses sight of the priority of the transcendent and spiritual realities which are premises of eschatological salvation" (RM 20). By acting in this manner, the Church offers its specific participation to human development, which is the obligation of all.

158 The Church's social teaching is what the magisterium proposes on social matters. It contains principles, criteria, and guidelines for the activity of believers in the task of transforming the world in accordance with God's plan. Teaching the Church's social thought is "part of the Church's evangelizing mission" (SRS 41) and is "a valid instrument of evangelization" (CA 54) because it sheds light on how we are to live our faith.

2.1 Human Development: A Privileged Dimension of the New Evangelization

Jesus told his disciples to distribute the bread that had been multiplied to the **159** needy crowd, and thus "they all ate and were satisfied" (Mk 6:34-44). He cured the sick, and "he went about doing good" (Acts 10:38). At the end of time he will judge us by love (cf. Mt 25).

Jesus is the good Samaritan (cf. Lk 10:25-37), who embodies charity. Not only is he moved emotionally; he becomes real aid. His action is prompted by the dignity of every human being. The foundation for that dignity lies in Jesus Christ himself as creative Word (cf. Jn 1:3) made flesh (cf. Jn 1:14). In the words of the *Pastoral Constitution on the Church in the Modern World*: "In fact, it is only in the mystery of the Word incarnate that light is shed on the mystery of humankind. For Adam, the first human being, was a representation of the future, namely of Christ the Lord. It is Christ, the last Adam, who fully discloses humankind to itself and unfolds its noble calling by revealing the mystery of the Father and the Father's love" (GS 22).

This dignity was not lost through the wound of sin, but was raised up by God's compassion, which is revealed in the heart of Jesus Christ (cf. Mk 6:34). Hence, while Christian solidarity is certainly service to those in need, it is primarily fidelity to God. This is the basis for the intimate connection between evangelization and human development (cf. EN 31).

Our faith in the God of Jesus Christ and love for our brothers and sisters must **160** be translated into concrete deeds. Following Christ means being committed to live in his manner. This concern for consistency between faith and life has always been present in Christian communities. The apostle Saint James wrote: "What good is it, my brothers, if someone says he has faith but does not have works? If a brother or sister has nothing to wear and has no food for the day, and one of you says to them, 'Go in peace, keep warm, and eat well,' but you do not give them the necessities of the body, what good is it? So also faith of itself, if it does not have works, is dead" (Jas 2:14-17; 26).

The inconsistency between the faith professed and everyday life is one of the **161** causes of poverty in our countries. Christians have not known how to find in their faith the strength necessary to affect the criteria and decisions of those segments of society that provide ideological leadership and organize the common social, economic, and political life of our peoples. "Structures that cause injustice have been imposed on peoples who have a deeply rooted Christian faith" (*Puebla Conclusions,* 437).

162   As the Church's social teaching points out, development ought to lead man and woman from less human to ever more human conditions until they come to full knowledge of Jesus Christ (cf. PP 20-21). At its root, we discover that this teaching is a true hymn to life— to all life from that of the unborn to that of the outcast.

163   Mary, who became concerned over the need that arose at the wedding feast of Cana, is a model and figure of the Church in facing any kind of human need (cf. Jn 2:3ff). As he did with Mary, Jesus enjoins the Church to strive to show a motherly concern for humankind, and especially for those who suffer (cf. Jn 19:26-27).

2.2   The New Signs of the Times in the Realm of Human Development

2.2.1   Human Rights

164   The equal dignity of human beings because they are created in God's image and likeness is reinforced and perfected in Christ. In taking on our nature in the incarnation, and especially in his redeeming action on the cross, the Word demonstrates how much each person is worth. Therefore, Christ, God and man, is the deepest source assuring the dignity of the person and his or her rights. Every violation of human rights runs counter to God's plan and is sin.

165   In preaching the gospel—the deep root of human rights—the Church is not usurping a task foreign to its mission. On the contrary, it is obeying the command of Jesus Christ when he made aiding the needy an essential requirement of its evangelizing mission. States do not grant these rights; it is their role to protect and develop them, for they belong to human beings by their very nature.

Pastoral Challenges

166   -   Awareness of human rights has advanced considerably since Puebla, along with significant actions by the Church in this area. At the same time, however, the problem of the violation of some rights has grown, and social and political conditions have worsened. Ideologically motivated interpretations and manipulation by some groups have confused the meaning of human rights, and there obviously is a greater need for legal avenues and procedures for citizen involvement.

- Human rights are violated not only by terrorism, repression, and murder, **167** but also by the existence of conditions of extreme poverty and unjust economic structures that give rise to vast inequalities. Political intolerance and indifference toward the situation of widespread impoverishment indicate a contempt for the way people are actually living that we cannot pass over in silence.

- Violence against the rights of children, women, and the poorest groups in society (e.g., small farmers, indigenous people, and African Americans) are worthy of special condemnation. We must also condemn drug trafficking.

Pastoral Directions

- Promote human rights more effectively and courageously on the basis of **168** the gospel and the Church's social teaching, through word, action, and collaboration, by becoming committed to the defense of individual and social rights of the human being, of peoples, of cultures, and of the marginal sectors, as well as of those who are vulnerable or imprisoned.

- Be committed to defending life from the initial moment of conception to its last breath.

- Participate with discernment in agencies for dialogue and mediation as well as in institutions to support the various kinds of human rights victims, provided they are serious and are not engaged in manipulation by employing ideologies that are incompatible with the Church's social teaching.

- Strive resolutely in the light of gospel values to overcome all unjust discrimination based on race, nationalism, culture, gender, and creed by endeavoring to eliminate all hatred, resentment, and vindictiveness and by promoting reconciliation and justice.

2.2.2 Ecology

Creation is the work of the Word of the Lord and the presence of the Spirit, **169** who from the beginning was hovering over all that was created (cf. Gn 1-2). This was God's first covenant with us. When the human being who is called to enter into this covenant of love refuses to do so, sin affects the relationship with God and, likewise, with all creation.

Pastoral Challenges

- The United Nations Conference on the Environment and Development, held in Rio de Janeiro, has brought to the world's attention the gravity of the ecological crisis.

- Large Latin American cities are sick in their decaying downtown areas and especially in their shantytowns. In the countryside, indigenous and peasant populations are deprived of their lands, or they find themselves forced onto the least productive lands. They continue to slash and burn the forests in the Amazon and elsewhere on the continent. As a solution to this crisis, some are proposing sustainable development that seeks to respond to the needs and aspirations of the present without compromising the ability to deal with them in the future. The intent is thus to reconcile economic growth with ecological limits.

With regard to this proposal, we must ask whether all these aspirations are legitimate and who pays the cost of such development, as well as who it is intended to benefit. It cannot be a kind of development that gives preference to small groups at the expense of the world's great impoverished majorities.

- Development proposals must be subjected to ethical criteria. An ecological ethic entails abandoning a utilitarian and individualistic morality. It means accepting the principle that the goods of creation are destined for all and promoting justice and solidarity as utterly necessary values.

Pastoral Directions

- Since they belong to society, Christians are not free of responsibility for the development models that have brought about current environmental and social disasters.

- Undertake a task of reeducating everyone—starting with children and young people—on the value of life and the interdependence of the various ecosystems.

- Cultivate a spirituality that can recover the sense of God that is ever present in nature. Explain the new relationship established by the mystery of the incarnation, by which Christ assumed all that is created.

- Appreciate the new platform for dialogue created by the ecological crisis, and question wealth and waste.

- Learn from the poor to live in moderation and to share and esteem the wisdom of indigenous peoples on the preservation of nature as a *milieu* of life for all.

- Delve more deeply into the Holy Father's statements on the World Day **170** of Peace, especially within a context of "human ecology."

- Urge Christians to undertake dialogue with the North, through the channels of the Catholic Church as well as through ecological and ecumenical movements.

- In his love for the poor and for nature, Saint Francis of Assisi can be an inspiration for this path of reconciliation within creation and of human beings among themselves, which is a path of justice and peace.

2.2.3 The Earth: God's Gift

Christians look at the universe not simply as nature in isolation but rather as **171** creation and the Lord's first gift of love for us.

"The Lord's are the earth and its fullness; the world and those who dwell in it" (Ps 24:1) is the affirmation of faith that runs through the Bible and confirms our peoples' belief that the earth is the first sign of God's covenant with humans. Indeed, the biblical revelation teaches us that at creation the human being was placed in the garden of Eden to work it and care for it (cf. Gn 2:15) and use it (cf. Gn 2:16). Limits were pointed out (cf. Gn 2:17) to ever remind the human being that "God is the Lord and creator, that his is the earth and all it contains," and that the human being may use it, not as absolute master but as administrator.

These limits to the use of the land are intended to preserve the justice and right of all to partake in the goods of creation that God destined for the service of every human being who comes into this world.

In our continent, we have to take into account two opposed attitudes toward **172** the land, both of which differ from the Christian vision:

a) Within all elements that together form the indigenous community, the land is life, sacred space, and integrating center of community life. They live on the land and with it, and through it they feel in communion with their ancestors and in harmony with God. Hence, the land—their land—is a substantial part of their religious experience and of their own thrust in history. Indigenous people have a natural sense of respect for the land; it is mother earth who nourishes her children and thus, one must care for her, ask her permission to sow, and not mistreat her.

b) The commercial vision looks at the land exclusively in terms of exploitation and profit, even going so far as to drive off and forcefully expel its legitimate owners.

That same commercial attitude leads to speculation with urban property, making the land unavailable for housing for the ever-growing numbers of the poor in our large cities.

Besides these categories, we cannot forget the situation of small farmers who work their land and earn their families' livelihood using traditional technologies.

173   The attitude proper to the Christian vision is based on Sacred Scripture, which regards the land and the elements of nature primarily as allies of God's people and instruments of our salvation. Jesus Christ's resurrection once more sets humankind before the mission of liberating all of creation, which is to be transformed into a new heaven and a new earth, where righteousness will dwell (cf. 2 Pt 3:13).

Pastoral Challenges

174   -   The problematic situation of the land in Latin American and the Caribbean is a challenge to us, since "five centuries in which the gospel has been present... have not yet brought about an equitable distribution of the goods produced by of the land," which "is still unfortunately in the hands of small groups" (John Paul II, *Lenten Message,* 1992). For the most part, the former aboriginal peoples were stripped of their lands, while legislation made it difficult for African Americans to own land. Small farmers today bear the burden of institutional disorder and the consequences of economic crises.

    -    In recent years the impact of this crisis has been felt even more forcefully where the modernization of our societies has brought the expansion of international agribusiness, increasing integration between countries, greater use of technology, and a transnational presence. Very often these trends benefit the economically strong segments, but at the cost of small producers and workers.

- The situation of the tenure, administration, and utilization of land in Latin America and the Caribbean is one of the most pressing claims on human development.   **175**

Pastoral Directions

- Promote a change of attitude about the value of land on the basis of the Christian world view, which has connections with the cultural traditions of the poor and small farmers.   **176**

- Remind the lay faithful that they must influence the agrarian policies of their governments (especially their modernization policies) and peasant and indigenous organizations, so as to attain ways of using the land that are just, more community-oriented, and participatory.

- Support all those persons and institutions striving to bring governments and those who own the means of production to create a just and humane agrarian reform and policy, one that can legislate, plan, and provide support for a more just distribution of land and for utilizing it more efficiently.   **177**

- Support in solidarity those organizations of small farmers and indigenous people who are struggling through just and legitimate channels to hold onto or reacquire their lands.

- Promote those technical advances required to make the earth productive, while also keeping in mind market conditions and, accordingly, the need to develop an awareness of the importance of technology.

- Encourage theological reflection on the land question, stressing inculturation and an effective presence of pastoral agents in peasant communities.

- Support the organization of mediating groups, such as cooperatives, to serve as a means for the defense of human rights, democratic participation, and community education.

2.2.4   Impoverishment and Solidarity

178   Evangelizing means doing what Jesus Christ did in the synagogue when he stated that he had come to "bring glad tidings" to the poor. He "became poor although he was rich, so that by his poverty you might become rich" (2 Cor 8:9). He challenges us to give an authentic witness of gospel poverty in the way we live and in our church structures, just as he gave it.

Such is the basis for our commitment to a gospel-based and preferential option for the poor, one that is firm and irrevocable but not exclusive or excluding, as was very solemnly affirmed at the Medellín and Puebla Conferences. Like Jesus, we draw inspiration for all community and personal evangelizing activity from such a preferential option (cf. SRS 42 and RM 14; OA 16). The poor Church wants to energize the evangelization of our communities with the "evangelizing potential of the poor" (*Puebla Conclusions,* 1147).

Discovering the face of the Lord in the suffering faces of the poor (cf. Mt 25:31-46) challenges all Christians to a deep personal and ecclesial conversion. Through faith, we find faces emaciated by hunger as a result of inflation, foreign debt, and social injustice; faces disillusioned by politicians who make promises they do not keep; faces humiliated because of their culture, which is not shown respect and is sometimes treated with contempt; faces terrorized by daily and indiscriminate violence; anguished faces of the abandoned children who wander our streets and sleep under our bridges; suffering faces of women who are humiliated and disregarded; weary faces of migrants, who do not receive a decent welcome; faces aged by time and labor of people who lack even the minimum needed to survive decently (CELAM, *Working Document,* 163). Merciful love also means turning toward those who are in spiritual, moral, social, and cultural need.

Pastoral Challenges

179   -   The growing impoverishment in which millions of our brothers and sisters are plunged—to the point where it is reaching intolerable extremes of misery—is the cruelest and most crushing scourge that Latin America and the Caribbean are enduring. We condemned it at both Medellín and Puebla, and we are now doing so once again with concern and anguish.

-   Statistics eloquently indicate that during the last decade situations of poverty have increased in both absolute and relative numbers. As pastors, we are torn apart by the continual sight of the throng of men and women, children, youth, and the aged who endure the unbearable weight of dire poverty, as well as the various forms of social, ethnic, and cultural exclusion. They are specific unique human persons who find their horizons ever more closed and their dignity ignored.

- We look on the impoverishment of our people not simply as an economic and social phenomenon described and measured by the social sciences. We look at it from within the experience of many people whose daily struggle to live we share as pastors.

- Policies of a neoliberal type now prevailing in Latin America and the Caribbean further deepen the negative impact of these mechanisms. The gaps in society have widened as the market has been deregulated in an indiscriminate way; major portions of labor legislation have been eliminated and workers have been fired; and the social spending that protected working-class families has been cut back.

- We have to extend the list of suffering faces that we already noted at Puebla (cf. *Puebla Conclusions,* 31-39), all of them disfigured by hunger, terrorized by violence, aged by subhuman living conditions, and anguished over family survival. The Lord asks us to discover his own face in the suffering faces of our brothers and sisters.

- However, we are happy to note the numerous efforts that various groups and institutions in Latin America and the Caribbean are making to change this situation. The Church, which is called to be ever more faithful to its preferential option for the poor, has played a growing role in such efforts. For that we thank God, and we urge that the path already opened be widened, since there are many more who have yet to trod on it.

Pastoral Guidelines

- Assume with renewed decision the gospel-inspired and preferential **180** option for the poor, following the example and the words of the Lord Jesus, with full trust in God, austerity of life, and sharing in goods.

- Give priority to providing fraternal service to the poorest among the poor and helping institutions that take care of them: the handicapped, the sick, old people who are alone, abandoned children, prisoners, people with AIDS, and all those who need the merciful approach of the "good Samaritan."

- Examine personal and community attitudes and behaviors, along with pastoral structures and methods, so that rather than alienating the poor they may facilitate closeness and sharing with them.

- Foster social involvement vis-à-vis the state by demanding laws to defend the rights of the poor.

- Make our parishes a space for solidarity.

- Support and encourage those organizations for economic solidarity with which our people are trying to respond to their desperate situations of poverty.

- Press governments to respond to the hardships that are being worsened by the neoliberal economic model whose primary impact is on the poor. When considering these situations, it is important to single out the millions of Latin Americans who are struggling to survive in the informal economy.

2.2.5 Work

Given its humanizing and saving significance, the realm of work is one of the areas of greatest concern to us in our pastoral activity. Its origins lie in the human being's co-creative vocation as "image of God" (cf. Gn 1-26), and it has been rescued and elevated by Jesus, the worker and "carpenter's son" (cf. Mt 13:55 and Mk 6:3).

As custodian and servant of the message of Jesus, the Church has always seen human beings as subjects who dignify work, as they achieve their own fulfillment and bring God's work to perfection by making it a hymn of praise to the Creator and service to their brothers and sisters.

The constant teaching by the Church's magisterium that work is as it were the "key to the social question" has been confirmed in the recent social encyclicals of John Paul II (*Laborem Exercens; Sollicitudo Rei Socialis; Centesimus Annus*). That teaching particularly highlights "the subjective dimension" of work (LE 6), which is the most eloquent expression of the dignity of the worker.

Pastoral Challenges

- The situation today challenges us to develop a culture of work and **183** solidarity, based on faith in God the Father, who makes us brothers and sisters in Jesus Christ. In the realm of working people, we can observe the following: a decline in their living conditions and respect for their rights; little or no observance of what the law says should be done for the weakest sectors (e.g., children, pensioners, and so forth); a loss of the independence of workers' organizations due to dependencies or self-imposed dependencies of various kinds; abuse by capital, which is unaware of or denies the primacy of labor; few or no job opportunities for young people. It is obvious that there is an alarming lack of work or employment, with all the ensuing economic and social insecurity. Labor is calling for the economy to grow and productivity to increase so as to make possible greater welfare for individuals and their families through a just and fair distribution.

- The rights of working people are part of the moral patrimony of society, **184** and they should be protected by means of an adequate social legislation along with the judicial component that may be necessary for reliability and continuity in labor relations.

Pastoral Directions

- Foster and support pastoral work with labor in all our dioceses so as to **185** promote and defend the human value of work.

- Support organizations of working people to defend their legitimate rights, especially the right to adequate pay and to a just social protection for old age, illness, and unemployment (cf. CA 35).

- Encourage training for workers, business people, and government officials in their rights and duties and help provide places for meeting one another and working together.

2.2.6   Human Mobility

The Word of God becomes flesh in order to unite in a single people those who **186** were wandering dispersed and to make them "citizens of heaven" (cf. Phil 3:20; Heb 11:13-16).

Thus, God's son becomes a pilgrim and undergoes the experience of the displaced (cf. Mt 2: 13-23) as a migrant living in an insignificant village (cf. Jn 1:46). He trains his disciples to be missionaries by having them undergo the experience of migrants so that they will put their trust only in the love of God, whose good news they bear (cf. Mk 6:6b-12).

Pastoral Challenges

187 - In recent years, there is a sharp increase in migration to the two great countries in the north and also, albeit to a lesser extent, to better-off Latin American countries. We see new phenomena, such as the voluntary repatriation and the deportation of undocumented people. Increased travel and tourism and even religious pilgrimages and the needs of those who make their living at sea, all demand special care on the part of the Church.

- In those countries which for social and economic reasons are especially prone to migration there are generally no social measures to halt it; and in the receiving countries the tendency is to block entry. The serious consequences include family breakdown and the siphoning off of the productive forces of our own peoples, along with the uprooting, insecurity, discrimination, exploitation, and religious and moral degradation of the migrants themselves. Nevertheless, in some instances they manage to become part of Catholic communities and even to revitalize them.

Pastoral Directions

188 - Reinforce pastoral attention related to human movement by connecting efforts between dioceses and bishops conferences of the affected regions and by taking care that within the reception and other services provided for migrants, their spiritual and religious wealth be respected.

- Make government circles aware of the issue of migration so as to achieve equity in laws on labor and social security and compliance with international agreements.

189 - Offer migrants a catechesis adapted to their culture and legal aid to protect their rights.

- Present alternatives to small farmers so that they will not feel forced to migrate to the city.

2.2.7   The Democratic System

Christ the Lord, who was sent by the Father for the redemption of the world, **190** came to proclaim the good news and begin the reign and, through personal conversion, to bring about a new life according to God and a new kind of common life and social relationship. Faithful to the mission entrusted to it by its founder, the Church is to constitute the community of the children of God and to aid in building a society where the Christian values of the gospel are paramount.

The Church respects the legitimate autonomy of the temporal order and has no specific model for the political system. "The Church values the democratic system inasmuch as it ensures the participation of citizens in making political choices, guarantees to the governed the possibility both of electing and holding accountable those who govern them, and of replacing them through peaceful means when appropriate" (CA 46).

In recent years, the Church in Latin America and the Caribbean has played an active role in this process. In many countries, its activity has laid the groundwork for a common life based on dialogue and respect for the human person. Supported by the magisterium of its social teaching, the Church has been accompanying the people in their struggles and yearnings for greater participation and government based on the rule of law.

The people of our continent have been winning freedom, which indeed is **191** inherent in the human person and has been brought to the fore by modernity. Thus, it has been possible to establish democracy as the most accepted system of government, although its exercise is still more formal than real.

Pastoral Challenges

- In some countries democratic common life, which took root after **192** Puebla, has been deteriorating. The reasons include the following: administrative corruption, separation of party leadership from the concerns of the grass roots and the real needs of the community; a lack of program and disregard for the social, ethical, and cultural dimensions by party organizations; governments elected by the people but not truly directed toward the common good; a great deal of political patronage and populism, but little participation.

Pastoral Guidelines

193 - Proclaim persistently to civil society the values of a genuine pluralistic, just, and participatory democracy.

- Teach and urge the people really to become actively involved.

- Create conditions for lay people to learn the Church's social doctrine with a view to acting politically to remedy and improve democracy and truly serve the community.

- Provide guidance for the family, the school, and the various levels of the Church to educate in those values that provide the basis for genuine democracy: responsibility, shared responsibility, participation, respect for the dignity of persons, dialogue, and the common good.

2.2.8   New Economic Order

194 Conscious that a new economic order affecting Latin America and the Caribbean is taking shape, the Church is obliged to make a serious effort at discernment from its own perspective. We must ask ourselves: How far should the freedom of the market extend? What must be its features if it is to serve the development of the vast majority?

195 According to John Paul II's recent teaching (cf. the encyclical letter *Centesimus Annus*), the free activity of individuals in the market is legitimate. That does not mean that the market can provide all the goods that society needs nor that society can pay for many goods that are necessary. The market economy must keep these limits in mind.

Hence, the Holy Father's teachings point to the need for specific actions by governments so that the market economy will not become an absolute to which everything is sacrificed, thus aggravating inequality and the exclusion of the vast majority. There cannot be a creative and yet socially just market economy unless the whole society and the actors within it are firmly committed to solidarity through a legal framework that safeguards the value of the person, honesty, respect for life and distributive justice, and a real concern for the poorest.

Although by halting inflation and stabilizing the economy, economic **196** adjustments may be beneficial in the long run, they tend to produce a sharp drop in the living standards of the poor. The state, therefore, has the obligation to make up for the social costs to the poorest, within the limits of what is possible, but sincerely and generously.

The problem of the foreign debt is not only—or even primarily—economic; **197** rather, it is a human problem for it leads to an ever greater impoverishment and blocks the development and slows the advancement of those who are poorest. We ask ourselves whether the debt is valid, when paying it seriously jeopardizes the survival of our peoples, when the population was not consulted before contracting the debt, and when it has not always been used for lawful purposes. Hence, as pastors, we make ours the concern of John Paul II when he says that "it is necessary to find—and in fact is partly happening—ways to lighten, defer or even cancel the debt, compatible with the fundamental right of peoples to subsistence and progress" (CA 35).

Pastoral Challenges

- The eighties have been characterized by the scourge of inflation **198** augmented by fiscal deficit, the weight of foreign debt and monetary disorder, devastation of government finances due to the loss of revenue sources, inflation and corruption, and the drop in investment both domestic and foreign, along with other trends.

- Internationally, the ratio between prices for raw materials and finished goods has been increasingly unequal and discriminatory and has had a very negative effect on the economy of our countries. This situation still exists and is tending to become worse.

- Impoverishment and the accentuation of the gap between rich and poor **199** have a very serious impact on the vast majority of our peoples as a result of inflation and the lowering of real pay levels, the lack of access to basic services, unemployment, the growth of the informal economy, and scientific and technological dependence.

- A consumeristic and selfish mindset and life style—widely promoted by the media—are spreading, and they hinder or prevent a more just and decent way of organizing society.

- In response to the crisis of economic systems that has led to failures and frustrations, there is a tendency to propose a free market economy as the solution. Many understand it in terms of neoliberalism, and on the basis of narrow or reductive interpretations of person and society, they see it as extending beyond the purely economic sphere.

Pastoral Directions

200 - Fortify the knowledge, dissemination, and implementation of the Church's social teaching in various circles.

- Foster at various levels and in different sectors of the Church a social pastoral activity whose starting point is the gospel's preferential option for the poor, by being active through proclamation, denunciation, and witness, and by encouraging cooperative undertakings in the context of a market economy.

- Educate in the values of hard work and sharing, of honesty and austerity, of the ethical and religious sense of life so that starting in the family—the first school—new human beings may be formed to live in a more fraternal society, where people will experience that goods are meant for all, in the context of comprehensive development.

201 - Lay the groundwork for a real and efficient economy of solidarity, while assuring that socioeconomic models likewise be created on the local and national levels.

- Encourage the search for and implementation of socioeconomic models that combine free enterprise, personal and group creativity, and the moderating function of the state, while making certain to devote attention to those sectors that are most in need. All of this is to be aimed at achieving an economy of solidarity and participation, reflected in various kinds of property.

202 - Develop international economic relations that can facilitate technology transfer in an atmosphere of social reciprocity.

- Denounce those mechanisms of the market economy that do deep damage to the poor. We cannot fail to be present at a time when there is no one to watch over their interests.

203 - Bear in mind that the informal economy arises out of a need for survival, although it is vulnerable to illness, inflation, and so forth.

- Remind the lay faithful that they are to bring their influence to bear so that the government can achieve greater stability in economic policies, eliminate administrative corruption, and further extend decentralization in administration, the economy, and education.

- Acknowledge the basic role of the firm, the market, and private property, and the ensuing responsibility toward the means of production and human creativity in a legal framework of social justice (cf. CA 42).

2.2.9   Latin American Integration

Experience has shown that no nation can live and achieve solid development in isolation. We all feel the pressing need to bring together what is dispersed and to join our efforts so that interdependence may become solidarity, which in turn may be transformed into fraternity. Hence, these are the values that we single out in speaking about the economic and social reality of the world and of the yearnings for humanization latent in them.   **204**

Christians find very deep motivations for continuing this effort. Jesus Christ has made God's reign present: a reign of justice, love, and peace. He has made all of us brothers and sisters by becoming our brother and teaching us to recognize that we are children of one and the same Father (cf. Mk 14:36). He himself has called us to unity: "that they may all be one, as you, Father, are in me and I in you" (Jn 17:21).

The Church is conscious that it plays a unique role and that it has the task of developing a sense of being part of humankind and fostering a culture of solidarity and reconciliation.

It is characteristically human that nations and persons must be interdependent for the sake of a genuine solidarity. We also note that the worldwide trend of nations to associate with one another, which is a sign of the times, is likewise observable in Latin America and the Caribbean.   **205**

John Paul II has insisted on the need to transform structures that no longer meet the needs of peoples and particularly that, "Stronger nations must offer weaker ones opportunities for taking their place in international life" (CA 35). Observing the spectacle of countries that are ever richer alongside others that are ever poorer he said: "Solutions must be sought on a worldwide scale, by establishing a true economy of communion and participation in goods, on both international and national levels. In that regard, one factor   **206** that can make a notable contribution to overcoming the pressing problems today affecting this continent is Latin American integration. Those in charge of governments have a grave responsibility to promote the process—already underway—of integrating peoples whom a common geography, Christian faith, language and culture have already drawn together in the course of history" (OA 15).

Pastoral Challenges

207 - Our own nations find themselves isolated and splintered, at the very moment when the economy of the planet is undergoing globalization, and large blocs are being established or reestablished.

208 - The establishments of large blocs threatens to leave the whole continent to the extent that it does not respond to their economic interests.

- There is a breakdown within our countries as the result of discrimination against races or groups and of the economic, political, and cultural predominance of particular interests that also impede a broader opening.

- The same lack of communion between the local Churches of one nation to another, or between neighboring countries on the continent, weakens the integrating power of the Church itself.

Pastoral Directions

209 - Foster and accompany efforts to integrate Latin America as a "great homeland" from a perspective of solidarity, which further requires a new international order.

- Promote justice and participation within our nations by educating in those values, condemning situations that contradict them, and giving the witness of relating fraternally.

- Encourage initiatives and strengthen such structures and agencies for collaboration within the Church as may be necessary or useful, while respecting the various areas of authority. In this sense, take up the Holy Father's suggestion about a meeting of the episcopates from throughout the Americas.

2.3 The Family and Life: Especially Urgent Challenges in Human Development

2.3.1 The Family, Sanctuary of Life

With joy and conviction, the Church announces the good news with regard   **210**
to the family. In it the future of humankind is being forged, and it represents
the crucial frontier of the new evangelization. That is what we proclaim here
in Latin America and the Caribbean at a moment in history when the family
is suffering from many forces that are attempting to destroy or distort it.

Certainly, the most fitting place for speaking about the family is in
connection with the local Church, the parish, and ecclesial communities,
since the family is the domestic church. Due to the enormous problems
facing human life today, however, we are including this topic in the section
devoted to human development.

Of course, we acknowledge that there are different kinds of families in both
the countryside and the cities, each in its own cultural context. Everywhere,
however, the family is leaven and sign of divine love and of the Church itself,
and therefore it must be open
to God's plan.

As God originally disposed, marriage and family are institutions of divine   **211**
origin and not the result of human will. When the Lord says, "From the
beginning it was not so" (Mt 19:8), he is referring to the truth about marriage,
which according to God's plan rules out divorce.

Man and woman, being image and likeness of God (cf. Gn 1:27) who is love,   **212**
are called to live in marriage the mystery of trinitarian communion and
relationship. "God inscribed in the humanity of man and woman the
vocation, and thus the capacity and responsibility, of love and communion"
(FC 11). Man and woman are called to love in the totality of their body and
spirit.

Jesus Christ is the new covenant; in him, marriage reaches its true grandeur.   **213**
A model for every family was established through his incarnation and his
family life with Mary and Joseph in their home in Nazareth. Through Christ,
love between spouses becomes like his: total, exclusive, faithful, and
fruitful. With the coming of Christ and by his intention, as the apostle
proclaims, marriage does not merely return to its original perfection but it
is enriched with new content (cf. Eph 5:25-33). Christian marriage is a

sacrament in which human love is sanctifying and communicates divine life through the work of Christ; a sacrament in which the spouses signify and embody the love of Christ and his Church, a love that travels the road of the cross, of limitations, forgiveness, and failings in order to arrive at the delight of resurrection. It must be kept in mind that "a valid matrimonial contract cannot exist between baptized people without its being by that very fact a sacrament" (CIC 1055:2).

214 In the plan of God, Creator and Redeemer, the family discovers both its identity and its mission: to protect, reveal, and communicate love and life through four fundamental responsibilities (cf. FC 17):

a) The mission of the family is to live, grow, and improve as a community of persons characterized by unity and indissolubility. The family is the privileged site for personal fulfillment together, alongside those one loves.

b) To be "sanctuary of life" (CA 39) and serve life, since the right to life is the foundation of all human rights. Such service is not limited to mere procreation, but is real help for transmitting and educating in genuinely human and Christian values.

c) To be the "primary and vital cell of society" (FC 42). By its nature and vocation, the family should foster development and be an advocate for policies that truly favor families.

d) To be a "domestic church" receiving, living, celebrating, and proclaiming God's word; it is a sanctuary where holiness is built up, and from which the Church and the world can be made holy (cf. FC 55).

Despite the grave crisis of the family, we note that many Latin American and Caribbean families are full of hope and faithful to the plan of God, Creator and Redeemer. They are struggling to embody fidelity, openness to life, the Christian education of their children, and commitment to the Church and the world.

215 God is the very Lord of life. Life is God's gift. The human being is not, and cannot be, the arbiter or master of life. Families must responsibly accept a child as a most precious and unique gift from God. The conceived unborn child is the poorest, most vulnerable and most defenseless being and must be defended and guarded. Today, it is even more obvious that birth control and abortion are connected both objectively and subjectively. The unitive significance of the conjugal act is sharply cut off from its procreative meaning, thus betraying the very meaning of love.

2.3.2 Challenges Confronting the Family and Life Today

- Historical and cultural change has had an impact on the traditional **216** image of the family. Couples living together, divorce, and abortion are increasingly common. What is new is that these family problems have become an ethicopolitical problem, partly has a result of a "secularizing" mindset and of the media.

- The fact that marriage and the family have been proposed by God, who **217** invites man and woman, who have been created out of love, to carry out his loving project in fidelity to death, is too often ignored due to the prevailing secularism and psychological immaturity, as well as for socioeconomic and political reasons. All these factors lead to the breakdown of the moral and ethical values of the family itself. The upshot is the painful reality of broken families, couples in irregular unions, the growth of civil matrimony without a sacramental celebration, and unmarried couples living together.

- A growing number of families in Latin America and the Caribbean **218** represent a challenge to governments, society, and international agencies by reason of their situation of dire poverty and hunger due to unemployment, the lack of decent housing and of schooling, sanitation, and low pay; and by reason of the abandonment of old people and the growing number of single mothers.

- The culture of death is challenging us. As human beings we are **219** saddened, and as Christians we are concerned to be witnessing campaigns against life spreading through Latin America and the Caribbean and disrupting the attitude of our people with a culture of death. Selfishness, fear of sacrifice and the cross, combined with the hardships of modern life are causing a rejection of the child, who is not welcomed in the family with responsibility and joy, but is regarded as an aggressor. A genuine "demographic terrorism" is used to instill fear in people by exaggerating the degree to which population growth may jeopardize quality of life.

There is a widespread distribution of contraceptives, most of which cause abortions. Large numbers of women are victims of mass sterilization programs.

Men are also falling prey to these threats. Our continent is suffering from "contraceptive imperialism, which entails imposing on peoples and cultures any kind of contraception, sterilization, and abortion considered effective with no respect for religious, ethnic, or family traditions of a people or a culture" (*Letter* of the Holy See to the WHO [World Health Organization] Meeting in Bangkok).

The massacre of abortion grows greater every day and is producing millions of victims in our peoples of Latin America. Besides being prenatal euthanasia, such an anti-life attitude leads to the elimination of newly born children and of the old and sick, who are regarded as useless, defective, or a "burden" for society. Other expressions of the culture of death are euthanasia, war, guerrilla warfare, kidnapping, terrorism, and drug trafficking.

220   -   The Christian faithful are confused when they see contradictions and inconsistency on the part of those working in family pastoral work who they do not follow the Church's magisterium (*Humanae Vitae; Familiaris Consortio; Reconciliatio y Poenitentia*).

221   -   Latin America and the Caribbean have a growing child population. Children, adolescents, and young people make up more than half the continent's population (55%). This "silent emergency" in Latin America and the Caribbean is a challenge not only from a numerical standpoint, but especially from a human and pastoral standpoint. Indeed, in many cities there is a growing number of "street children," who wander about day and night with no home and no future. In some countries, they have suffered campaigns waged by police and private groups to wipe them out; there are children with no family, no love, no access to education—in other words, children in extreme physical and moral misery, often as the result of family breakdown. We even observe a grotesque buying and selling of boys and girls, a traffic in organs, and even children used for devil worship. From the standpoint of education in their faith, there is a notable neglect of reception of the sacraments and catechesis.

2.3.3   Pastoral Directions

222   1. Emphasize the priority and centrality of family pastoral work in the diocesan Church. Pastoral agents must be trained for that purpose. The apostolic movements directed at marriage and the family can offer valuable cooperation to local Churches, within a comprehensive plan.

- Family pastoral work cannot be limited to a merely protective stance; it must be forward-looking, bold, and positive. It must discern with gospel wisdom the challenges that cultural changes pose to the family. It must condemn violations against justice and the dignity of the family. It must stand by families from the poorer segments in the countryside and the cities and promote their solidarity.

- Family pastoral work must take care to train future spouses and to accompany spouses, especially during the first years of their married life. Courses to prepare engaged couples before the marriage ceremony have proven their worth.

2. Proclaim that God is the only Lord of life, and that the human being is not, and cannot be, master or arbiter of human life. Condemn and reject any violation by the authorities on behalf of birth control, euthanasia, sterilization, and deliberate abortion. Likewise, condemn and reject the policies of some governments and international agencies that condition economic aid on anti-life programs. **223**

Seek, following the example of the Good Shepherd, approaches and ways of carrying out a pastoral work aimed at couples in irregular situations, especially divorced women, and those who have remarried civilly. **224**

Strengthen the life of the Church and society on the basis of the family: enrich it with family catechesis, prayer in the home, the eucharist, participation in the sacrament of reconciliation, and knowledge of God's word, in order to be leaven in the Church and society. **225**

3. Invite theologians, scholars, and Christian married couples to work together with the hierarchical magisterium in order to clarify the biblical grounds, ethical motivations, and scientific reasons for responsible parenthood, and for deciding freely in accord with a well-formed conscience and with the principles of morality, both with regard to the number of children one can educate and the methods in keeping with a genuine responsible parenthood. The fruit of such research will be the promotion of programs and services to make known natural methods of family planning and to prepare manuals for education about sexuality and love, aimed at children, adolescents, and young people. **226**

- In response to the efforts of certain demographic programs, we must recall the Holy Father's words in his opening address to this Conference: "What is needed is to augment resources and distribute wealth with greater justice so that all may participate equitably in the goods of creation" (OA 15).

227   4. Exercise the Church's prophetic mission by condemning any assault against children whether born or unborn. Make known and urge compliance with the "Convention on the Rights of the Child" along with the observations of the Holy See, as well as the letter of the Holy See, *On the Rights of the Family*. Guide lay people to promote in the various countries legislation to protect the rights of the child and press for compliance. Accompany and truly support parents, educators, catechists, and religious congregations devoted to educating children, with special attention to growth in the faith. Foster a mystique for working on behalf of children and promoting pastoral work with children, through prophetic and charitable actions that testify to Christ's love for the poorest and most abandoned children.

Chapter 3

CHRISTIAN CULTURE

Introduction

The coming of the Holy Spirit at Pentecost (cf. Acts 2: 1-11) makes manifest **228** the universality of the commission to evangelize: the aim is to reach every culture. It also makes manifest the cultural diversity of the faithful when they hear the apostles speaking, each in his own language.

Culture arises with God's initial command to human beings: to grow and multiply, to fill the earth and subdue it (cf. Gn 1:28-30). Thus, culture means cultivating and expressing the full range of the human in a loving relationship with nature and in the community dimension of peoples.

When through the incarnation Jesus Christ assumes and expresses everything human except sin, the Word of God enters into culture. Jesus Christ is thus the measure of everything human, including culture. He who took flesh in his people's culture, brings to each culture in history the gift of purification and plenitude. All the cultural values and expressions that can be oriented to Christ foster what is genuinely human. What does not go by way of Christ will not be redeemable.

Through our radical adhesion to Christ in baptism, we have been committed **229** to strive so that faith—fully proclaimed, thought, and lived—may become culture. Thus, we may speak of a Christian culture when a people's shared sense of life has been so permeated that the gospel message has been placed "at the basis of its thinking, its fundamental principles of life, its criteria for judgment, and its norms for activity" (OA 24), and from there "is projected into the 'ethos' of a people . . . its institutions and all its structures" (OA 20).

This evangelization of culture, which reaches into its dynamic core, is expressed in the inculturation process, which John Paul II has called the "center, means, and aim of the new evangelization" (*Address to the Interna-*

tional Council on Catechesis, September 26, 1992). Authentic Christian values, discerned and assumed in faith, are necessary in order to incarnate the gospel message and the Church's reflection and practice into that culture.

The Virgin Mary is with the apostles when the Spirit of the risen Jesus enters and transforms those peoples from different cultures. Mary, who is the model for the Church, is also a model for the evangelization of culture. She is the Jewish woman who represents the people of the old covenant with all its cultural reality. However, she opens herself to the newness of the gospel and is present in our lands as common mother, both of the native peoples and of those who have come here. From the outset, she encourages the fresh cultural synthesis that constitutes Latin America and the Caribbean.

Inculturation of the Gospel

230   Since we stand before "a cultural crisis of unsuspected dimensions" (OA 21) in which gospel values and even basic human values are vanishing, the Church is presented with an enormous challenge, that of undertaking a new evangelization. We propose to respond to this challenge with the effort to inculturate the gospel. The gospel must be inculturated in the light of the three great mysteries of salvation: Christmas, which demonstrates the path of the incarnation and prompts evangelizers to share their lives with the evangelized; Easter, which leads through suffering to the purification of sins, so that they may be redeemed; and Pentecost, which by the power of the Spirit enables all to understand the wonders of God in their own language.

The inculturation of the gospel is a process that entails recognizing those gospel values that have been maintained more or less pure in present-day culture and recognizing those new values that are congruent with the message of Christ. The aim of inculturation is to bring society to discover the Christian nature of those values, to esteem them, and to maintain them as values. It also seeks to incorporate gospel values that are not present in the culture, either because they have been obscured or have even disappeared. "Through inculturation, the Church makes the gospel incarnate in different cultures and at the same time introduces peoples, together with their cultures, into her own community" (RM 52). By becoming incarnate in these cultures, faith seeks to correct their errors and prevent syncretism. Inculturating the faith is a task proper to local Churches, under the direction of their pastors and with the participation of the whole people of God. "Properly applied, inculturation must be guided by two principles: compatibility with the gospel and communion with the universal Church" (RM 54).

3.1 Cultural Values: Christ, Standard for Our Moral Behavior

-   Created in God's image, we find the standard for our moral behavior in **231**
    Christ, Word made flesh, and fulfillment of the human being. Natural
    ethical activity, which is essentially connected to human dignity and the
    rights that follow from it, is the foundation for a dialogue with nonbe-
    lievers.

Through baptism, we are born into a new life and are enabled to approach
our model, who is Christ. Christian morality means journeying toward him;
that is the way of life proper to the believer, who with the aid of sacramental
grace follows Jesus Christ, lives the joy of salvation, and overflows with
expressions of charity for the life of the world (cf. Jn 15; OT 16).

-   Conscious of the need to continue along this journey, the Christian
    strives to form his or her own conscience. The development and wealth
    of peoples is dependent on doing so both individually and collectively,
    and on the maturity of their attitude, their sense of responsibility, and the
    purity of their customs (cf. OA 19). Christian morality is only under-
    stood within the Church, and it reaches fulfillment in the eucharist.
    Everything we can offer in the eucharist is life; what cannot be offered
    is sin.

Pastoral Challenges

-   In Latin America and the Caribbean many people still remain faithful to **232**
    Jesus Christ, thank God, even in adverse circumstances. Nevertheless,
    in our societies there is an obvious growing ethical and moral gap, and
    more specifically we note a distortion of conscience, a permissive
    ethics, and a notable decline in the sense of sin. Faith has a declining
    influence; esteem for religion is on the wane; and God is not acknowl-
    edged as supreme good and final judge. The practice of the sacrament
    of reconciliation is declining. The Church's official moral teaching is
    presented inadequately.

-   Corruption is widespread. Public funds are mismanaged; demagoguery, **233**
    populism, and the "political lie" during election campaigns are on the
    rise; justice is mocked, impunity is becoming commonplace, and the
    community feels impotent and defenseless against crime. The result is
    a growing social insensitivity and skepticism when justice is not done,

and laws contrary to fundamental human and Christian values are passed. The goods of the earth are not distributed fairly; nature is abused; and the ecosystem is being damaged.

234 - Birth control campaigns, genetic manipulation, the abominable crime of abortion, and that of euthanasia all foster an anti-life attitude and actions. Life comes to mean the conquest of the weak by the strong, thereby encouraging actions of hatred and destruction and preventing human fulfillment and growth.

235 - Thus, it is clear that the dignity of the human person is being increasingly undermined. The culture of death, violence and terrorism, drug addiction and drug traffic are growing. The wholeness of human sexuality is being debased, as men and women and even children are turned into an industry of pornography and prostitution; within the overall atmosphere of permissiveness and sexual promiscuity, the terrible evil of AIDS is spreading, and venereal disease is on the rise.

236 - What is called the "civil" or "citizen ethics" is being introduced as a norm of morality. It is based on a minimum consensus of all with the prevailing culture, with no need to respect natural morality and Christian standards. We can observe a "situation morality" that holds that something inherently evil would cease to be so in accordance with the persons, circumstances, or interests that may be at stake. The media often echo all such criteria and disseminate them.

Pastoral Directions

237 - Work to develop a Christian conscience and restore what has been lost in Christian morality. Become aware once more of sin (of both original sin and personal sins) and of God's grace as strength to enable us to continue to follow our Christian conscience. Awaken in all the experience of the love that the Holy Spirit pours into our hearts as the strength of all Christian morality.

238 - Exercise vigilance so that the media will neither be manipulative nor manipulated into transmitting, under the guise of pluralism, what destroys the Latin American people. Strengthen the unity of the family and its influence in the formation of moral conscience.

239 - Present the moral life as the following of Christ, with the emphasis on

practicing the beatitudes and frequently participating in the sacraments. Communicate the moral and social virtues, so as to make us new human beings and creators of a new humankind. This proclamation must be vital and *kerygmatic,* especially where secularism has made greater inroads. Catechesis should present Christian behavior as the genuine following of Christ. Take care to assure that the proper application of criteria of degree in moral matters not diminish the demanding requirements of conversion.

- Encourage ongoing formation for bishops and priests, deacons, men and women religious, lay people, and especially pastoral agents, in keeping with the teaching of the magisterium. The liturgy should express more clearly the moral commitments it entails. Popular religiosity should be oriented toward conversion, especially at devotional shrines. Approach to the sacrament of reconciliation should be encouraged and made easier. **240**

- With regard to drug problems, encourage preventive action in society and attention and care for drug addicts; courageously condemn the harm that drug addiction and drug traffic wreak on our peoples and the very serious sin entailed in their production, commercialization, and consumption. Point out in particular the responsibility borne by the powerful consumer markets. Encourage national and international solidarity and cooperation in combatting this scourge. **241**

- Guide and pastorally accompany those who build society to develop a moral conscience with regard to their tasks and their political activity. **242**

- Ever be open to dialogue with those who conduct their lives on the paths differing from those of Christian ethics. Commit ourselves truly to achieving the justice and peace of our peoples.

3.2 Unity and Plurality of Indigenous, African American, and *Mestizo* Cultures

Theological Perspectives

- Through the Spirit, God's action is continually at work within all cultures. In the fullness of time, God sent his Son, Jesus Christ, who assumed the social and cultural conditions of peoples and has truly become one of us "in every way, yet without sin" (Heb 4:15; cf. GS 22). **243**

- The analogy between the incarnation and the Christian presence in the sociocultural and historic context of our peoples leads us to pose the question of inculturation in theological terms. Such inculturation is a process conducted on the basis of the gospel from within each people and community by means of language and symbols that are comprehensible and that the Church regards as appropriate.

- One goal of inculturated evangelization will always be the salvation and integral liberation of a particular people or human group, strengthening its identity and trusting in its specific future. At the same time, it will stand opposed to the powers of death by taking on the perspective of Jesus Christ incarnate, who out of weakness, poverty, and the redeeming cross, saved humankind. The Church defends the genuine human values of all peoples, especially of those who are oppressed, defenseless, and excluded as they confront the overwhelming power of the structures of sin manifested in modern society.

Pastoral Challenges

244 - Latin America and the Caribbean constitute a multiethnic and multicultural continent on which indigenous, African American, and *mestizo* peoples and those descending from Europeans and Asians live together. Each has its own culture, which provides it with its own social identity in accord with each people's world vision, but they seek unity on the basis of their Catholic identity.

245 - The indigenous peoples of today cherish very important human values, and as John Paul II says, they hold the "belief that evil is identified with death and good with life" (*Message to Indigenous People*, 2). Those values and convictions derive from "the seeds of the Word," which were already present at work in their ancestors, enabling them to go on to discover the Creator's presence in all his creatures: the sun, the moon, mother earth, and so forth (cf. Ibid.).

From its first encounters with these native peoples, the Church sought to accompany them as they struggled for survival out of the unjust situation of people who had been defeated, invaded, and treated as slaves, and it taught them the way of Christ the Savior. Along with enormous suffering, the first evangelization brought major accomplishments and attained valuable pastoral insights. Their fruit has lasted to the present.

246 - African American cultures in Latin America and the Caribbean are

marked by a continual resistance to slavery. These peoples, who number in the millions, also have in their cultures human values that express the presence of God the Creator.

- It is true that during the first four centuries several million Africans were brought as slaves. They were violently torn away from their lands, separated from their families, and sold as items of merchandise. The enslaving of blacks and killing of Indians were the worst sin of the West's colonial expansion. Unfortunately, some baptized people were involved in slavery, racism, and discrimination.

- As the *Puebla Conclusions* state forcefully, in those peoples that are the **247** fruit of racial mixing, there has taken shape a particular *mestizo* culture in which popular religiosity, as an inculturated form of Catholicism, is very much alive. Nevertheless, the failure to observe Christian obligations stands side-by-side with admirable examples of Christian living, and ignorance of church teaching stands alongside Catholic experiences rooted in gospel principles.

- The cultural and religious expressions of peasants and people in outlying urban areas reflect a great deal of the continent's Christian legacy and a faith rooted in the values of God's reign.

Pastoral Directions: Inculturated Evangelization

After having joined the pope in asking forgiveness of our indigenous and **248** African American brothers and sisters "before God's infinite holiness for everything . . . that has been marked with sin, injustice, and violence" (*General Audience* [October 21, 1992], 3), we intend to carry out an inculturated evangelization:

1. *Toward Our Indigenous Brothers and Sisters*

- Offer the gospel of Jesus with the witness of a humble, understanding, and prophetic attitude, esteeming what they have to say through a respectful, frank, and fraternal dialogue; strive to learn their languages.

- Acquire greater critical knowledge of their cultures in order to appreciate them in the light of the gospel.

- Foster an inculturation of the liturgy by appreciating and drawing on those symbols, rituals, and religious expressions of theirs that are compatible with the clear meaning of the faith, while maintaining the value of the universal symbols and in harmony with the Church's general discipline.

- Accompany their theological reflection by respecting their cultural formulations, which help them to provide a reason for their faith and hope.

- Acquire greater knowledge of their world vision, which makes the complex of God-human-world a unity that pervades all human, spiritual, and transcendent relationships.

- Promote within the indigenous peoples their own native cultural values by means of an inculturation of the Church so as to embody God's reign more fully.

249 2. *Toward Our African American Brothers and Sisters*

Conscious of the problem of exclusion and racism weighing down on the black population, the Church in its evangelizing mission wishes to share in their sufferings and to accompany them in their legitimate aspirations for a more just and decent life for all (cf. Ibid.).

- Hence, the Church in Latin America and the Caribbean wants to support African American peoples in defending their identity and in acknowledging their own values, and to help them to keep alive those practices and customs of theirs that are compatible with Christian teaching (cf. *Message to African Americans,* 3).

- We likewise commit ourselves to devote special attention to the cause of African American communities in the pastoral field by encouraging the manifestation of the religious expressions proper to their cultures (cf. Ibid.).

250 3. Develop *mestizo* consciousness not only of racial amalgamation [*mestizaje*] but also of the cultural amalgamation that is typical of the majority of the people in many of our countries, for it is connected to the inculturation of the gospel.

Human Development of Ethnic Groups

In the interest of genuine human development, the Church wants to support **251** the efforts that these people are making to bring national and international law to recognize them as peoples with full rights to land and to their own organizations and ways of life, in order to safeguard their right to live in accordance with their identity, speaking their own language and observing their ancestral customs, and to establish relations with all the peoples of the earth on an equal footing.

Therefore, we take on the following commitments:

- Overcome the mindset and practice of development imposed from outside, and replace it with self-development so that these people may be artisans of their own destiny.

- Contribute effectively to slowing and halting policies that tend to cause indigenous cultures to vanish through forced integration or, at the other extreme, polices that seek to keep indigenous people isolated and excluded from the nation.

- Press for full respect for the human rights of indigenous and African American people, including their legitimate defense of their lands.

- As a specific gesture of solidarity with peasants, indigenous people, and African Americans, support the *Populorum Progressio* Foundation established by the Holy Father.

- Thoroughly reexamine our education systems in order to eliminate once and for all any trace of discrimination in teaching methods, sums invested, or in where they are invested.

- Do everything possible to guarantee to indigenous people and African Americans an education adequate to their particular cultures, beginning with bilingual literacy training.

3.3 New Culture

3.3.1 Modern Culture

Situation

252 - Although Latin America and the Caribbean are multicultural, they are deeply marked by Western culture, whose memory, consciousness, and aspirations are ever present in our prevailing common way of life. That is why modern culture has had such a great impact on the way we are, and why its postmodern period now opens other possibilities to us.

- The characteristic features of modern culture are the centrality of the human being; the values of personalization, of the social dimension, and of shared life; the absolutizing of reason, whose triumphs in science, technology, and information processing have satisfied many human needs. These same triumphs of reason have led to an attempt to be autonomous vis-à-vis nature, which is under its domination; autonomous vis-à-vis history, for which human beings now assume responsibility; and even autonomous vis-à-vis God, who is of no concern or who is relegated to personal consciousness, while only the temporal order is regarded as important.

- Postmodernity is the product of the failure of the reductionistic pretension of modern reason. It leads humankind to question some of the gains of modernity, such as trust in unlimited progress, although it also recognizes its positive features, as indeed the Church itself does (cf. GS 57).

- Both modernity, with its positive and negative features and postmodernity, insofar as it is a space open to transcendence, present serious challenges to the evangelization of culture.

Pastoral Challenges

253 - Cleavage between faith and culture insofar as modern human beings rule out transcendence and as a result of overspecialization, which makes it difficult to see the whole.

- Little awareness of the need for a true inculturation as the way to evangelize culture.

- Lack of correspondence between the values of the people which take their inspiration from Christian principles and social structures that cause injustice, preventing human rights from being exercised.

- The ethical vacuum and the prevailing individualism, which reduce the basis for values to a merely subjective consensus in society.

- The enormous power of the media, which often promote negative values.

- The fact that the Church is scarcely present in the area of the major expressions in art; in philosophical, anthropological, and social thought; and in the realm of education.

- The new urban culture, with its values, expressions, and characteristic structures; with its space at once open and diversified; with its mobility; and its predominantly functional relationships.

Pastoral Directions

- Present Jesus Christ as paradigm for every attitude, personal and social, **254** and as answer to the problems afflicting modern cultures: evil, death, lovelessness.

- Intensify dialogue between faith and science, faith and expressions, faith and institutions, which are major realms of modern culture.

- Exercise care for the signs and cultural language that points to the Christian presence and that makes it possible to introduce the originality of the gospel message into the heart of cultures, especially in the realm of the liturgy.

- Develop and train the laity to exercise their threefold function in the world: the prophetic function in the area of the word, thought, and their expression and values; the priestly function, in the world of celebration and sacrament, enriched with expressions, art, and communication; the royal function in the world of social, political, and economic structures.

- Encourage knowledge and discernment of modern culture with a view toward adequate inculturation.

3.3.2   The City

Pastoral Challenges

255 -   Today, Latin America and the Caribbean are in the midst of a rapid urbanization process. The post-industrial city is not merely a variant form of the traditional human habitat but, indeed, represents the passage from rural culture to urban culture, which is the location and driving force of the new universal civilization (cf. *Puebla Conclusions,* 429). In the city, the very way human beings in a social group, a people, or a nation, cultivate their relationship with themselves, with others, with nature, and with God is changing.

-    By the very nature of city, relationships with nature are almost always limited to the process of producing consumer goods. Relationships between persons become largely functional. Relations with God undergo a pronounced crisis because the mediation of nature, which is so important to rural religiosity, is now gone and because modernity itself tends to enclose the human being within the immanence of the world. Relations of urban people with themselves also change because modern culture leads people to prize especially their freedom, their autonomy, scientific, and technological rationality, and, in general, their subjectivity, their human dignity, and their rights. Indeed, the major centers creating modern science and technology are in the city.

-    However, our Latin American metropolitan centers are also typically surrounded by belts of poverty and misery. They almost always make up the bulk of their population and are the result of exploitive and excluding economic models. The spread of communication and transportation is leading to the urbanization of the countryside itself.

-    Today's city person is different in type from the rural person: he or she trusts in science and technology; is influenced by the media; is energetic and oriented toward what is new; is consumption-oriented, audiovisual, absorbed in the anonymous masses, and uprooted.

Pastoral Directions

256 -   Carry out a kind of pastoral work inculturated into the city in the areas of catechesis, liturgy, and the way the Church is organized. The Church should inculturate the gospel into the city and in the urban person.

Discern the positive and negative features of such persons; grasp their language and their symbols. The inculturation process encompasses the proclamation, assimilation, and reexpression of the faith.

- Reshape the urban parish. The Church in the city must reorganize its **257** pastoral structures. The urban parish must be more open, flexible, and missionary, allowing for transparochial and supraparochial pastoral activity. Indeed, the city structure demands a pastoral approach devised specifically for it. The large cities, where new forms of culture and communication emerge, ought to be privileged sites for mission.

- Encourage the training of lay people for urban mission, through biblical **258** and spiritual formation; create ministries conferred on lay people in order to evangelize large cities.

- Multiply small communities, ecclesial movements and groups, and Chris- **259** tian base communities. Undertake what has been called the "ministry of buildings" through the activity of committed lay people living in them.

- Organize a pastoral activity aimed at particular circles and functions that **260** is differentiated in accord with city spaces. A ministry of welcome to deal with migration. A ministry for marginal groups. Assure that the religious needs of the inhabitants of large cities receive attention during the summer months and vacations; strive to provide pastoral attention for those who habitually spend their weekends outside the city, where they are unable to fulfill their Sunday obligation.

- Encourage the evangelization of influential groups and those who are **261** responsible for the city in the sense of making it a decent habitat for people, and especially in the vast poor neighborhoods.

- Promote meetings and courses on the evangelization of large cities on **262** the continental (CELAM), national, and regional levels.

3.4 The Church's Educational Activity

Theological Perspectives

- We reaffirm what we have said at Medellín and Puebla (see *Medellín* **263** *Conclusions,* "Education"; and *Puebla Conclusions*); with that as a starting point, we indicate some aspects that are important for Catholic education today.

- Education is the assimilation of culture. Christian education is the assimilation of Christian culture. It is the inculturation of the gospel into culture itself. It takes place on a wide variety of levels: in school and outside; elementary and higher; formal and nonformal. In any case, education is a dynamic lifelong process of the person and of peoples. It gathers the memory of the past, teaches how to live the present, and projects toward the future. Hence, Christian education is absolutely necessary in the new evangelization.

264 - Christian education develops and strengthens in Christians their life of faith and assures that for them living truly means Christ (cf. Phil 1:21). Hence, the "words of eternal life" (Jn 6:68) sound within them, the "new creation" is brought about in each of them (cf. 2 Cor 5:17), and the Father's plan to sum up all things in Christ is carried out (cf. Eph 1:1-10). Thus, Christian education is based on a true Christian anthropology, which means the opening of human beings to God as Creator and Father, toward others as brothers and sisters, and toward the world as what has been entrusted to them, not to exercise over it a despotic control that destroys nature but in order to develop its potential.

265 - No teacher educates without knowing why and toward what he or she is educating. In every educational project there is a human project; whether or not that project is of value depends on whether it builds or destroys the one being educated. That is its educational value. When we talk about a Christian education, we are saying that the teacher is educating toward a human project in which Jesus Christ lives. Education covers many aspects that are part of the project of educating a human being; many values are involved, but these values are never alone; they are always organized into an ordered whole, either explicitly or implicitly. If Christ is the foundation and end of that ordering, such an education is summing up everything in Christ and is a true Christian education. Otherwise, education may talk about Christ but it is not Christian.

- The Christian teacher should be regarded as an active member and representative of the Church who evangelizes, catechizes, and educates in a Christian manner. He or she has a defined identity in the church community. His or her role should be recognized in the Church.

- Currently, we find a series of values that are both challenging and ambivalent. Hence, arises the need to confront these new values in education with Christ, who reveals the mystery of the human being. In the new education, there is an effort to make the person grow and mature in accord with the demands of such new values. Moreover, they must be harmonized with what is specific to the Latin American context. **266**

- On the basis of secularistic criteria, we are generally expected to educate a person to be technically oriented, someone who is ready to dominate the world and live in an exchange of goods produced under certain political norms—as few as possible. This situation emphatically challenges us to be conscious of all the values present in it, and to be capable of summing them up in Christ; it challenges us to continue the direction of the incarnation of the Word in our education and to arrive at the project of life for every human being, namely Christ dead and risen.

Pastoral Challenges

- The situation of education in Latin America challenges us from other angles as well. We are challenged by the exclusion of many people from even basic school education and by the high degree of illiteracy in a number of our countries; by the crisis of the family, the primary educator, and by the divorce between the gospel and culture; by the social and economic differences that make a Catholic education, especially at higher levels, a heavy burden for many people. We are likewise challenged by the informal education received through so many communicators who are not really Christian (e.g., on television). **267**

- The Catholic university and the university of Christian inspiration is a great challenge since its task is particularly that of developing a human being as understood in Christian terms. Hence, it must be in a living, ongoing, step-by-step dialogue with humanism and with technological culture in order to know how to teach the true Christian wisdom in which the model of "worker" is joined to that of "sage" and culminates in Jesus Christ. Only thus will it be able to point to solutions to the complex unresolved problems of the emerging culture and the new social configurations, such as the dignity of the human person; the inviolable rights of life; religious freedom; the family as the first site for social commitment; solidarity on its various levels; the commitment proper to a democratic society, the complex economic and social question; the phenomena of the sects; the speed of cultural change. **268**

269 - Another challenge that arises with regard to schools in a number of countries is the thorny problem of relationships between state education and Christian education. Although these relationships have become easier in some countries, in other countries it is still not understood that a Catholic education is an inalienable right of Catholic parents and their children, and the resources necessary for that aid are not made available, or it is simply prohibited.

270 - Other significant challenges are the religious ignorance of young people, nonschool education, and informal education. Another challenge is that of an education apt for different cultures, and particularly indigenous and African American cultures, not only in the sense that it be in keeping with their own way of life but also that it not cut them off from progress, from equal opportunity, and from being able to build national unity.

Pastoral Directions

271 - Our commitments in the field of education can no doubt be summed up as pastoral work aiming at inculturation: education is the systematic means for evangelizing culture. Therefore, we take a stand for a Christian education based on life and on behalf of life in the individual, family, and community spheres and in the sphere of the ecosystem; education that fosters the dignity of the human person and true solidarity; and education incorporating a process of civil and social formation inspired by the gospel and the Church's social doctrine. We commit ourselves to an evangelizing education.

272 - We support parents in choosing the kind of education they want for their children in keeping with their convictions, and we condemn all intrusions of the civil power restricting this natural right. It ought to guarantee each person's right to religious formation and, therefore, the right to religious teaching in schools at all levels.

273 - We offer encouragement to Christian educators who work in church institutions, those congregations who continue to work in education, and Catholic teachers working in non-Catholic institutions. We must promote ongoing formation for Catholic educators so that they may be able to grow in their faith and in the ability to communicate it as true wisdom, above all in Catholic education.

274 - There is a pressing need for a true Christian formation on life, love, and

sexuality to correct the distortions of certain information received in schools. Education toward freedom is also a pressing need, since it is one of the fundamental values of the person. Christian education must also be concerned with education for work, particularly in the circumstances of contemporary culture.

- The charisms of the religious orders and congregations serving Catholic education in the various local Churches of our continent are of very great help for fulfilling the commission that we have received from the Lord to go and teach all nations (cf. Mt 28: 18-20), especially by evangelizing culture. We call on the religious men and women who have abandoned this extremely important field of Catholic education to return to their task. We also note that the "preferential option for the poor" includes the preferential option for the means to enable people to escape from their poverty, and that one of the privileged means for doing so is Catholic education. The preferential option for the poor is also made manifest when teaching religious continue to carry on their educational work in the many rural areas that are both remote and in great need.   **275**

- We must also make efforts that Catholic school education on all levels be within the reach of all people, and not be reserved for just a few, even while keeping in mind the economic problems involved. The responsibility of the parish community in the school and in its management should be developed. We ask that the public funds apportioned for Catholic education be guaranteed.   **276**

- In particular, we believe that on the basis of the apostolic constitution *Ex Corde Ecclesia*, the Catholic university is called to carry out an important mission of dialogue between the gospel and cultures and of advancing human development in Latin America and the Caribbean.

- Conscious of the worldwide extension of contemporary culture, we will form a critical consciousness toward the media on every level of Catholic education. There is a pressing need to provide effective criteria to prepare the family to use television, press, and radio.   **277**

- Transform the Catholic school into a community that is a radiating center of evangelization, through students, parents, and teachers. We are striving to strengthen the educational community and, in it, the process of civic and social formation, taking inspiration from the gospel and from the Church's social teaching so that it may respond to the true needs of the people. Thus, organizations of students, educators, parents, and alumni will be strengthened as a method of civil, social, and political   **278** education that may make open the way to the democratic formation of persons. We likewise ask governments to continue to direct their efforts to make education ever more democratic.

3.5   Social Communication and Culture

Theological Perspectives

279   -   Evangelization, the proclamation of the reign, is communication in order that we may live in communion (cf. *Puebla Conclusions,* 1063): "what we have seen and heard we proclaim now to you, so that you too may have fellowship with us; for our fellowship is with the Father and with his Son, Jesus Christ" (1 Jn 1:3). Every person and every human group develop their identity as they meet others (*otherness*). Such communication is the path that must be taken in order to come to communion (*community*). The reason is that the human being has been made image of the Triune God, and in the heart of revelation, we find God's trinitarian mystery as the eternally interpersonal communication, whose Word becomes dialogue, enters into history through the Spirit, and thus initiates a world of new encounters, exchanges, communication, and communion. This communication is important not only in the world but within the Church.

-   In the Father's gesture of communication through the Word made flesh, "the word becomes liberating and redemptive for all humankind in the preaching and activity of Jesus. This act of love through which God reveals himself in conjunction with humankind's response of faith brings about a deep dialogue" (Pontifical Council on the Mass Media, pastoral instruction, *Aetatis Novae*, 6). Thus, Christ is the model for the communicator: in him the wholly Other God comes forth to meet us and to await our free response. This encounter of communion with God is always growth. It is the way of holiness.

-   Thus, there is a very close relationship among evangelization, human development, and culture, which is based on communication. The Church thereby has specific tasks and challenges in the area of the media. That is what the pope said in his *Opening Address* to this Conference: "It must certainly be one of your priorities to intensify the Church's presence in the world of the media" (OA 25).

-   We know that we are in a new culture of the image and that the gospel message must be inculturated into this culture, thus making it expressive of Christ, who is the utmost communication. We understand the importance of the vast number of electronic means that we now have at our disposal for announcing the gospel. We thank God for granting us this new gift in contemporary culture.

Pastoral Challenges

- Technological advances in the area of communication, particularly in   **280**
  television, offers evangelization extensive possibilities for communicating with the most diverse levels and enables society to be interconnected around the globe. That is the positive feature, but in the current context it also presents very serious challenges, given the secularistic orientation of much programming.

- We are aware of how the communications industry has developed in Latin America and the Caribbean. It reflects the growth of economic and political groups that concentrate ownership of the various media into the hands of a powerful few. They come to manipulate communication, imposing a culture that encourages hedonism and consumerism and tramples our cultures along with their values and identities.

- We see how advertising often introduces false expectations and creates false needs. We also see how television programming in particular is full of violence and pornography, which aggressively make their way into the bosom of the family. We also note that the sects are continually intensifying and expanding their use of the media.

- Moreover, the Church's presence in the media world is still insufficient, and there are not enough workers with proper training to face the challenge. Moreover, the various episcopacies do not have adequate planning for pastoral work in the media.

- Telecommunications and information processing are new challenges to the integration of the Church into this world.

Pastoral Directions

- Support and energize the efforts of all those who in their use of the media   **281**
  are defending their cultural identity, by taking on the challenge of meeting new and different situations and striving to assure that an authentic dialogue takes place. Connect mass communication with

community and group communication. Strive to have our own media and, insofar as possible, a video production unit to serve Latin America and the Caribbean.

282 - Help to discern and guide communication policies and strategies. Their aim should be to enable persons to encounter one another so that an authentic and responsible freedom of expression may be in effect, to foster people's own cultural values, and to seek Latin American integration.

283 - Give Catholic media professionals enough support so that they can carry out their mission. Strive for a growing relationship of ecclesial communion with international organizations (e.g., OCIC-AL, UNDA-AL, UCLAP) "whose members can be valuable and competent collaborators of the bishops conferences and of individual bishops" (Pontifical Council on the Media, pastoral instruction, *Aetatis Novae,* 17). The episcopal commissions on the media in each country and DECOS-CELAM and SERTAL should augment and improve their presence in this field.

284 - Every effort should be made to assure that all pastoral agents working in and with the media be prepared technically, doctrinally, and morally. Likewise, there must also be an education plan aimed at critical perception, especially in homes, and at the ability to utilize the media and their language actively and creatively by employing our people's cultural symbols.

285 - Catholic universities must be encouraged to provide the highest quality human, academic, and professional media training. The languages and corresponding techniques of communication are to be taught in seminaries and houses of religious formation so as to assure sufficient systematic preparation.

Today, it is absolutely essential to use computers and information science to optimize our resources for evangelization. Progress must be made in installing the Church's information network in the various bishops conferences.

286 - Catholic publishing houses are to act in a coordinated manner within planned comprehensive pastoral activity.

Part III

JESUS CHRIST
LIFE AND HOPE OF
LATIN AMERICA
AND THE CARIBBEAN

PRIMARY PASTORAL DIRECTIONS

We have come to Santo Domingo from our local Churches. We brought "the joys and the hopes, the griefs and the anxieties" (GS 1) of our peoples. Yearnings that our continent have life and hope came with us. **287**

Our meeting with the Holy Father confirmed us in faith, hope, and love for the Lord and for the Church. The spiritual company of so many brothers and sisters who prayed for us and offered us their support gave us strength.

Daily celebration of the eucharist, meditation on God's word, and the work we did together with our trust placed in the Lord enabled us to experience truly the presence of Jesus in our midst (cf. Mt 18:20) and the action of the Spirit.

"Jesus Christ, the same yesterday, today, and forever" (Heb 13:8) has made us feel that he makes us "new creatures," (cf. 2 Cor 5:17); that he gives us "life . . . abundantly" (Jn 10:10); that he promises us "eternal life" (Jn 6:54). He is "our hope" (1 Tm 1:1).

We now return to our various fields of ministry. We will proclaim the gospel of life. We will continue to give a "reason for our hope" (1 Pt 3:15) to every single person whom the Lord sets on our paths.

As we conclude our reflections, with our hearts grateful to God, we turn to look over the work we have done in order to identify the main lines of pastoral work that we found and in order to continue our journey, guided by the three topics that the Holy Father invited us to study, deepen, and apply, starting here in this Fourth Conference. **288**

Looking back at our journey, we proclaim with new ardor our faith in Jesus Christ, Son of the Living God, sole reason for our life, and source of our mission. He is the Way, the Truth, and the Life. He gives us the life that we wish to communicate fully to our peoples so that all may have a spirit of solidarity, reconciliation, and hope.

We make this profession of faith under the protection of Our Lady of Guadalupe, patroness of Latin America, who has been with us in this episcopal gathering, and who is ever with us in the mission that the Lord entrusts to us. **289**

290 We renew our intention to further the pastoral guidelines, set by Vatican II, which were applied at the General Conferences of Latin American Bishops at Medellín and Puebla, and bring them up-to-date by means of the pastoral guidelines laid down at this Conference.

291 We regard the three topics that the Holy Father proposed to us as the three major pastoral directions that we assume for our Churches. Within the Santo Domingo guidelines, each local Church and each bishops conference will be able to find the challenges and pastoral directions that best meet its specific needs.

292 In the name of our local Churches in Latin America and the Caribbean, we commit ourselves to working on:

1. A new evangelization of our peoples.

2. A comprehensive development of our Latin American and Caribbean peoples.

3. An inculturated evangelization.

- In this sense, we now highlight those elements that received special emphasis during the conference and were approved in order to specify the three main pastoral directions and impel them forward.

1. A New Evangelization of Our Peoples

293 1.1. *The commitment involves everyone and arises out of living communities.* Lay people have a special role to play as the guidelines of the apostolic exhortation *Christifideles Laici* have stated. Among lay people, we once more invite young people to be a force of renewal in the Church and of hope for the world, as the pope has continually pleaded.

In order to raise up priests, permanent deacons, men and women religious, and members of secular institutes to take part in the new evangelization, we will encourage a vigorous vocational work.

294 1.2. *We are all called to holiness* (cf. LG 39-42). In a Church that is a missionary community, we must strive firmly for ongoing education of the faith through catechesis, whose foundation is the Word of God and the teaching authority of the Church, and which enables Catholics to give reasons for their hope at every moment vis-à-vis the sects and the new religious movements.

The celebration of faith in the liturgy, the summit of the Church's life, must be carried out joyfully and in a way that makes possible a more lively and active participation that is committed to the situation of our peoples.

1.3. *This is the missionary moment in the Americas.* We heartily and **295** enthusiastically invite all to take part in evangelization, not only within our Churches but beyond our borders. That will be our response to the example of missionaries who came to the Americas from other lands to communicate their faith to us. It will also be a source of generosity for our young people and a blessing for our Churches.

2. A Comprehensive Human Development for the Peoples of Latin America and the Caribbean

2.1. *We make ours the cry of the poor.* In continuity with Medellín and **296** Puebla, we assume with renewed ardor the gospel preferential option for the poor. This option, which is neither exclusive nor excluding, will, in imitation of Jesus Christ, shed light on all our evangelization activity.

With that light, we urge the development of a new economic, social, and political order in keeping with the dignity of each and every person, fostering justice and solidarity, and opening horizons of eternity for all of them.

2.2. *We say yes to life and to the family.* Facing very serious assaults on life **297** and the family, which have intensified in recent years, we propose a firm action to defend and promote life and the family, which is the "domestic church" and sanctuary of life, from its conception to the natural end of its temporal stage. All human life is sacred.

3. An Inculturated Evangelization

This is the third commitment that we assume in the perspective of new methods and expressions for living the gospel message today.

3.1. *Large cities in Latin America and the Caribbean, with their many* **298** *problems, have challenged us.* We will devote attention to evangelizing these centers where most of our population now lives. Our care will also extend to rural areas; they already feel the impact of cultural changes.

299 3.2. *We want to come close to indigenous and African American peoples* so that becoming incarnate in their cultures, the gospel may manifest all its vitality and they may enter into the dialogue of communion with other Christian communities for the sake of mutual enrichment.

300 3.3. *We will likewise seek to stimulate an effective educational activity* and a steadfast effort at modern communication.

301 We place ourselves under the impulse of the Holy Spirit, who has been leading the Church in love since Pentecost. He granted us the grace of Vatican Council II and our General Conferences in Rio de Janeiro, Medellín, and Puebla.

We are certain that we will enjoy the help of the Spirit so that, as we leave Santo Domingo, we will continue even more united among ourselves, and under the guidance of the Holy Father, successor to Peter, and despite our limitations, we will be able to project enthusiastically the proclamation of Jesus Christ and his reign over Latin America and the Caribbean.

The Church in Latin America and the Caribbean proclaims its faith: **302**

"JESUS CHRIST: YESTERDAY, TODAY, AND FOREVER" (cf. Heb. 13:8)

Our local Churches, united in hope and love,
under the protection of Our Lady of Guadalupe,
in communion with the Holy Father
and in continuity with the pastoral directions given
at the general conferences held at Medellín and Puebla
commit themselves to work toward:

1. A New Evangelization of Our Peoples

-   To which *all* are called.

-   With emphasis on *encouraging* vocations with particular involve ment by *lay people*, and among them, by *young people*.

-   Through ongoing education in the faith and its celebration: *cate-chesis and liturgy.*

-   Also beyond our borders: *missionary* Latin America.

2. A Comprehensive Development of the People of Latin American and the Caribbean

-   Out of a renewed gospel preferential option for the poor.

-   At the service of *life* and the *family.*

3. An Inculturated Evangelization

-   That can permeate environments characterized by *urban culture.*

-   That can take flesh in *indigenous and African American cultures.*

-   With an effective educational activity and modern communica-tions.

PRAYER

Lord Jesus Christ, Son of the Living God,
Good Shepherd, and our Brother.
Our only option is for You.

United in love and hope
under the protection of our Lady of Guadalupe,
Star of Evangelization, we pray for your Spirit.

Grant us the grace
so that, in continuity with Medellín and Puebla,
we may heartily carry out a new evangelization
to which we are all called
with special involvement by lay people,
and particularly youth,
committing ourselves to an ongoing education of faith,
celebrating your praise,
and proclaiming you beyond our own borders
in a firmly missionary Church.
Increase our vocations
so that there may be laborers for your harvest.

Encourage us to be committed
to promote a comprehensive development
of the Latin American and Caribbean people
out of a gospel-inspired and renewed
preferential option for the poor
and at the service of life and the family.

Help us to work
toward an inculturated evangelization
that may permeate the *milieux* of our cities
and may take flesh in indigenous and African American cultures
through an effective educational activity
and modern communications.

Amen.

INDEX

ABANDONED: those who are, 85.

ABORTION: evil of in Latin America, 9; affects woman's dignity, 110; connection to contraception, 215; contraceptives that also cause abortion, 219; millions of victims, 219; condemnation, 223; anti-life, 234.

ABUSES: against indigenous people, 20; sexual, 112.

ADDICTION: 241.

ADOLESCENCE (ADOLESCENTS): presence of vocations in, 82; Jesus went through, 111; maturing emotionally, 112; reaction to consumerism and suffering, 112; formation in faith, 115; room for participation of, 119; pastoral youth work aimed at, 119; presenting a Jesus who is attractive, 119; educational process of, 120; numerous in Latin America, 221.

ADVERTISING: negative effects of, 280.

AFRICAN AMERICANS: vocations, 80; abuses against dignity of, condemned, 107; encouraging measures so that they may have a decent life, 110; pastoral youth work aimed at, 119; religions, 137; violation of rights of, 167; did not have access to land, 174; part of Latin America, a multiethnic continent, 244; the Church recognizes values of, 249; pastoral care of, 249.

AFRICANS: slaves in Latin America and the Caribbean, 20; violently torn away from their lands, 246.

AGRARIAN REFORM: 177.

AIDS: 235.

ALCOHOLISM: 112.

ANTI-BIRTH ATTITUDE: 234.

APOSTLES: Holy Spirit poured forth on, 7; Christ's mandate to them, 23; task and witness of, 33; present in base communities, 61.

APOSTOLIC ASSOCIATIONS: their emergence prompted by the Holy Spirit, 102; their legitimacy, 102; can become closed in on themselves, 102.

APOSTOLIC MOVEMENTS: multiplying in the Church, 38; contribution to new evangelization, 48; mission of the parish in, 58; should welcome pastoral work with families, 64; a sign of the times, 95; Holy Spirit inspires their emergence, 102; basic elements of, 102; can become enclosed on themselves, 102; should be coordinated within joint planned pastoral activity, 102; struggle on behalf of women, 108; in mission to the nations, 125; causes of growth, 148; multiplying in cities, 259.

ART: *mestizo*, 18; not guided by gospel criteria, 96; little presence of the Church in, 253.

ATHEISM: 21.

BAPTISM: entry into the reign of God, 5; renews human dignity, 13; baptized people have not become aware that they belong to the Church, 26, 33, 96, 97, 130; holiness received, 37; conversion, renewal of baptism, 46; contemplative dimension, 47; makes us God's people, 65; consequence of, 94; ministries conferred on laity from baptism, 101; divine filiation, 121; taken on in a missionary spirit, 131; taking pastoral advantage when people present children for, 131; radical adhesion to Christ in, 229; we are born to a new life in, 231.

BEATITUDES: adhering to their proclamation, 5; lived by new people in Latin America and the Caribbean, 32; moral life, 239.

BIBLE: 38, 49, 108, 135.

BIRTH CONTROL: programs, 110.

BISHOPS: preside over particular churches, 11; prophetic stance of denunciation during the conquest, 20; agent of new evangelization, 25; in the unity of the local Church, 55; represented by the parish priest, 58; communion of Christian base communities with, 61, 63, 64; essential to the Church's activity, 67; ongoing formation for, 69; 73; relationship and communion of religious with, 91, 93; promote vocations, 128.

BODY AND BLOOD OF CHRIST: 6.

BREAKDOWN: in the family, 79; 187; inside our countries, 208.

BUDDHISM: 147.

CALL: to enter the reign, 4; to conversion, 24, 32; to live as community of faith, 61; to ordained ministers, 67; to holiness, 78; to priestly service, 79; to task of evangelization, 94; to live the priestly, prophetic, and royal function, 94; to be active agents of the new evangelization, 97.

CATECHESIS: as a pastoral means, 19; as a prophetic ministry of the Church, 33; importance of, 41; *kerygmatic* and missionary, 49; of conformation and its connection to vocation, 80; collaboration with lay people, 101; continues education in the faith, 130; purpose of, 142; aimed at migrants, 189; family, 225; presents Christian behavior as genuine following of Christ, 239; means for continuing education of faith, 302.

CATECHISMS: 49.

CATECHISTS: African Americans, 19; effort and sacrifice of, 41; with solid knowledge of the Bible, 49.

CATHOLICS: often ignorant of truths about Jesus, 39; some do not feel as Church, 96.

CELAM: scope of, 69; training courses, 84; ecumenism section, 135; conferences and courses on evangelization of large cities, 262.

CELEBRATION OF FAITH: instrument of evangelization, 19; one of the purposes of the liturgy, 35; present in pastoral concern, 36; expresses commitment to the Lord, 43; presence of Christ, 51; carried out in community, makes present the events of Jesus' life, 52; mission of the parish, 58; in culture of young people, 117; adapting it to cultures, 151; should reach people's lives, 156.

CHARISMS: from the Holy Spirit for the new evangelization, 23; integration into the new evangelization, 57; at the service of comprehensive pastoral work, 64; conferred by Jesus for benefit of all, 65; keeping them alive in religious communities, 91; to foment creativity, 101; proper to religious orders and congregations, 275.

CHARITY: pastoral, in the new evangelization, 28; component of Christian worship, 34; in holiness, 37; made manifest in the sacraments, 45; in priestly commitment, 72; in the pastoral activity of women religious, 90; linked to evangelization, 257.

54, 55, 58, 68, 85, 92, 128; rich in ministries, 66; living and operational through the sacraments, 67; needs priest models, 72; led by the vowed woman, 90; made up primarily of lay people, 94; activity of lay people in, 102, 103, 105; called to stand alongside life, 106; its concerns, 131; promotes dialogue, 136; is community-oriented and participatory, 142; accusations against, 146; role in defending human rights, 165; custodian and servant of Jesus' ministry, 182; respects autonomy of temporal order, 190; active role in society, 190; 204; announces the good news on the family, 210; defends the values of peoples, 243; has accompanied Latin American peoples since discovery, 245, 249.

CITIES: features of large, 255; post-industrial, 255; relation to nature, 255; pastoral structures of the urban church, 257; challenges evangelization, 298.

CIVILIZATION OF LOVE: 61, 120.

CLERICALISM: 43.

CLIENTELISM: 192.

COLLEGIALITY: of bishops, 68.

COLONIAL PERIOD: 20.

COMLAS: 125.

COMMERCIAL VISION: of land, 172.

COMMISSIONS: national, of clergy, 73; of bishops, for communication, 283.

COMMITMENT: missionary, of the Church, 23, 27, 292, 302; to human development, 35, 157; personal and community, to the Lord, 43; priest's, to the new evangelization, 72; basis of vocational pastoral work, 80; of religious in local Church 92; some Catholics do not assume, 96; of lay people in new evangelization, 98, 103; of young people 115; in daily life, 118; to justice and peace, 242; in education, 271; of all the faithful, 293.

COMMUNICATION: proclamation of God's reign, 279; of the Father through the Son, 279; basis for the relationship between evangelization and human development, 279; Mass, to community and groups, 281; policies and strategies for, 282; modernization, 300; aid for new evangelization, 302.

COMMUNION: of human being with God, 5; of all beings with God, 5; between Christians, 6; in apostolic faith, 8; between priests and bishops, 11; in heaven, 14; in small communities, 48; experienced in communities in the continent, 54; in the local Church, 55; need to advance toward, 56; stimulated and guided by the parish, 58; of leaders with the parish priest and the bishop, 61; sincere search in communities, 62; of pastoral agents with parish priest, 63; of bishops with the pope, 67; among pastors, 68; among ordained ministers, 69; service of pastors, 74; in Latin America, 75; of religious with the bishops, 93; of lay councils, 98; feature of universal Church, 143; lacking between local Churches, 208; with international organizations, 283.

CONFIRMATION: experience of the grace of the Spirit, 46; gives rise to ministries conferred on lay people, 101; give special attention to this sacrament, 115; assume it in a missionary way, 131; opportunity to present the newness of Jesus Christ, 131.

CONQUERORS: 20.

CONQUEST AND COLONIZATION: 20.

CONSCIENCE: in the conversion of the Church, 30; cultivation of moral conscience, 156; distortion of in the growing ethical and moral gap, 232; work on its formation, 287.

CONSISTENCY BETWEEN FAITH AND LIFE: 44, 48.

CONSUMERISM: causes, 44; reaction of young people and adolescents to, 112; spread by media, 199; feature of contemporary urban people, 254.

CONTEMPLATION: 37; including it in pastoral plans, 144.

CONTEMPLATIVE LIFE: 37, 86.

CONTRACEPTIVES: their connection to abortion, 215; massive distribution of, 219.

CONVERSION: demand for entering God's reign, 5; frees from the powers of death, 9; continual process in the Church, 23; call of new evangelization, 24; demand of new evangelization, 30; call to members of the Church, 32; initial, 33; work of the Holy Spirit, 40; fruit of proclamation of Jesus, 46; relationship with ongoing formation, 72; in sects, 147; action of the gospel message, 157; challenge that springs from discovery of the poor and suffering, 178.

CORRUPTION: evil present in Latin America, 9; leads to deterioration in some countries, 192; feature of the 1980s, 198; influence of lay people to end, 203; has become widespread, 233.

COUNCILS: priests, 69, 73; pastoral, 98; of lay people, 98.

COUNSELS: evangelical, 37

COVENANT: renewal of in Latin America, 16; with religious and missionaries, 85; creation was the first, 169.

CREATION: transformed by Jesus Christ, 14; relationship with plan of redemption, 157; work of the Word of the Lord, 169; first gift of God's love, 171.

CREATIVITY: in presenting the gospel, 29; in establishing ministries and services, 101; encouraging it in celebrations of faith, 117.

CRISIS: social, 149; ecological, 169; of economic systems, 199; of the family, 214, 267; of culture, 230.

CROSS OF CHRIST: present in the Americas, 2; in the inhabitants of Latin America, 3; connection with following him, 10; Holy Spirit gives strength to carry, 40.

CULTURAL CHANGES: response of new evangelization to, 26; influence on young people, 79.

CULTURE OF DEATH: features of, 9, 26; the challenge of, 219, 235.

CULTURES: permeated by the gospel, 1; identified with Mary, 15; of the Americas encountering Iberian, 18; gospel present at its core, 21; of the image, 29; means for arriving at 29; urban emerging, indigenous and African American, 30; task of theologians, 33; inroads of secularism, hedonism, and communism in, 44; of reconciliation and solidarity, 77, 183, 204; vocations coming from, 80; indigenous and African American, 84; 246; 302; laity prominent in, 99; 103; birth of, 229; consensus of all with the prevailing culture, 236; *mestizo*, 247; Latin American marked by Western, 252; 254; emerging 268.

DAY OF THE LORD: 43; 51.

DECENTRALIZATION: administrative, economic, and educational, 203.

DEGRADATION: 197.

DEMAGOGUERY: 187.

DEMOCRACY: military to serve, 99; Church's appreciation for, 190, 191; values of, 193; remedying and improving, 193; educating in the values of, 193; 253.

DEPENDENCE: scientific and technological, 199.

DEPORTATION: of the undocumented, 187.

DEVELOPMENT: promoted by evangelization, 13; in human advancement, 157; introduced from outside, 251; in communications, 280.

DEVOTION: to Mary in vocational work, 80; in the eucharist, 143.

DIALOGUE: between gospel and culture, 22; with modernity and the postmodern, 24; between theologians and pastors, 33; between pastors and lay councils, 98; between man and woman, 109; theological-ecumenical, 135; with non-Christian religions, 137, 138; obstacles, 137; with African American and indigenous religions, 138; created by the ecological crisis, 169; with the north, 170; with indigenous people, 248; between faith and conscience, 254; with those responsible for the media, 281.

DIGNITY OF THE HUMAN PERSON: its measure in Jesus Christ, 8; given by the vigor of proclamation of Christianity, 13; defended by the great evangelizers, 20; arises from the acceptance of the Holy Spirit, 24; returned to contemporary human being by Jesus Christ, 27; in the Church's social teaching, 157; motivates Jesus' activity, 159; derives from creation of human being in God's image, 164; now being degraded, 235; in universities, 268; fostered in education, 271.

DIOCESES: not enough pastoral agents, 56; base communities should be integrated into, 63; religious connected to, 68; comprehensive pastoral activity, 80; apportionment of their human and material resources, 114.

DISCRIMINATION: overcome it in the light of the gospel, 168; consequence of migration, 187; in the Church, 246.

DIVINATION: 155.

DIVISIONS: in local Churches, 68; among Christians, 133.

DIVORCE: ruled out by God's plan, 211; ever more common, 216.

DOMESTIC SERVANTS: 110.

DRUG ADDICTION: 9, 235, 241.

DRUG TRAFFICKING: 112, 167, 219, 235, 241.

ECOLOGY: defense of ecological balance, 138; forests cleared, 169; relationship with economic growth, 169.

ECONOMIC MODELS: neoliberal, 181; for the sake of human beings, 201; exploiting and excluding, 255.

ECONOMY: human being should not be subordinated to it, 27; not guided by gospel criteria, 96; of solidarity, 102; neoliberal economic model, 181; market, 195; economic adjustments, 196; informal, 199; free market, 200; of participation, 201; stability and decentralization, 203; globalization, 207.

ECUMENISM: 133, 135.

EDUCATION: pastoral means during the first evangelization, 19; immediate pastoral objective, 99; new languages and symbols, 109; does not respond to the needs of youth, 112; participatory and transforming experience, 119; to see God in history, 156; lack of educational services, 218; of indigenous and African Americans; 251; Catholic, 263, 264; role of teacher, 265; secularist criteria for, 266; many people left out, 267; challenges of, 269, 270; pastoral directions, 271, 272, 274, 275, 276, 277; orientation, 284; of faith, 294, 302.

EDUCATIONAL PROGRAMS: 109.

EPISCOPAL CONFERENCES: reexamine and reshape church structures 69; can find challenges and pastoral directions in this document, 291.

EQUALITY: of man and woman, 104, 109; between human beings, 164.

ETHICS: in a society that is secular and indifferent, 154; relationship to development, 169; civil or citizens, 236; Christian, 242; ethical vacuum, 253.

EUCHARIST: sacrament of Christ's love 6; gathers faithful and pastors,

11; expression of commitment, 43; source of unity of local Church, 55; foundation of pastoral work for vocations, 80; experience of unity, 123; shows the unity of the Church, 143; enriched by catechesis, 225.

EUTHANASIA: 219, 223, 234.

EVANGELIZATION: Church's reason for being, 12; promotes comprehensive human development, 13; example in Blessed Juan Diego, 15; first, in Latin America, 16, 24; inspired by the Holy Spirit, 19; source of its power, 27; showed show the demands of Jesus, 48; based on experiences of God, 91; commitment of lay people, 98; role of Mary and of women, 104; adapted to cultures, 151, 229, 248, 253; relationship to human development, 157, 279; goal, 243; challenges, 252; preparation for, 262; means proclaiming the reign, 279; commitment at Santo Domingo, 292, 297; of large cities, 298; 302.

EVANGELIZERS: some did not recognize the positive features of pre-Columbian cultures, 17; defended the rights and dignity of native people, 20; saints are the best, 28; religious, 85; laity called to be, 94.

EVIL: origins, 9; response, 254.

FAITH: arrival in Latin America, 16; separated from life, 24, 96, 161; loss of sense of, 26; robust and weak, 35; relation to holiness, 37; ignorance of in society, 39, 102, 156, 160; growth in, 54, 115; shared in mission to the nations, 125; casts light on earthly realities, 178; relationship with culture, 229, 230, 243.

FAITHFULNESS: to the Word, 27, 28, 72; to the magisterium, 33; to the Lord and to men and women, 67; in marriage, 217.

FAMILY: attacks on, 9, 297; mission of, 64, 101, 193, 214; woman's role in, 106, 109; as first school, 200; future of humankind forged in, 210; as domestic church, 210, 214; rural and urban, 210; divinely instituted, 211; home in Nazareth its model, 213; its identity, 214, promotes development, 214; crisis of, 214; change in its traditional image, 216; in situation of extreme poverty, 218; fortifies the life of society and the Church, 225; first space for social commitment, 268; new evangelization at its service, 302.

FISCAL DEFICIT: 198.

FIVE CENTURY ANNIVERSARY OF EVANGELIZATION: 2, 20, 21.

FOLLOWING JESUS: 5, 10, 13, 87, 160.

FOREIGN DEBT: 178; 197; 198.

FORMATION AND TRAINING: liturgical, 43, 51; of the laity, 44, 45, 57, 60, 61, 95, 96, 98, 99, 102, 103, 107, 115, 185, 237, 238; should be ongoing for ordained ministers, 69, 72, 73, 77, 240; of adolescents, 82; priestly and religious, 83, 84, 127, 128, 133, 135; of moral conscience, 242; of Catholic educators, 273; in universities, 284.

FREEDOM: derives from the truth, 32; military are to serve, 99; of association of laity, 100; peoples of Latin America are winning, 151; false response of pseudo-religious movements, 155.

GANGS: 112.

GAP BETWEEN RICH AND POOR: 199.

GENETIC MANIPULATION: 234.

GNOSTICS: 147.

GOD: chose a new people in Latin America, 2; love for human beings, 27; expects fruits of holiness from Church, 31; love for youth, 118; Father rich in mercy, 129; Lord and Creator, 171; Lord of Life, 215; 223.

GOD'S LOVE: made manifest in Jesus Christ, 4; for the poor and needy, 4; source of priestly life, 70.

GOOD NEWS: proclaimed by Jesus, 4; to the poor, 4; celebration of its being implanted in Latin America, 16; credibility for its acceptance, 28; Jesus asks us to proclaim it, 30; lay people called to proclaim, 94.

GOSPEL: proclaim it forthrightly, 13; experience fullness of, 21; life and hope spring from it, 23; one and unique, 24; in dialogue with modernity and the postmodern, 24; to reach all, 29; present it to the new cultural realities, 30, 60; religious manifest its power, 85, 91; transforms society, 98; light and hope, 107.

GRACE: frees us from the forces of death, 9; relationship with salvation, 12; saves through Jesus Christ in the Church, 45; received in baptism, 46; priestly ministry born from, 70; is strength to attain a Christian conscience, 237.

GROUPS: prayer, 38; apostolic, 58, 98, 259; youth, 120; missionary, 125; of families and Bible circles, 142; mediating, 177.

GROWTH IN THE NUMBER OF THE FAITHFUL: 2.

GUERRILLA WARFARE: 219.

HANDICAPPED: 180.

HEALING: 147, 149.

HEDONISM: 44, 280.

HINDUISM: 268.

HISTORY: forging a truly human, 24; Jesus Christ permeates 27; presence of evil in, 76; human beings assume, 252.

HOLINESS: of the Church, 31, 32, 38; contribution of theologians, 33; of church members, 37; possible by the action of the Spirit, 40; priestly, 70, 71; in lay people, 97; a call to all Christians, 99, 294; a priority of pastoral activity, 144.

HOLY SPIRIT: impulse of the new evangelization, 1; anoints Jesus Christ, 4; leads God's children, 10; gathers believers and pastors, 11; poured out over the peoples of Latin America, 16; awaited in pre-Colombian cultures, 17; inspires the work of evangelization, 19; new evangelization based on power of, 23; within cultures, 24; creative breath of the new evangelization, 27; ignites the heart of the Church, 28; inspires new methods, 29; sanctifies the Church, 32; must be preached, 40; received in baptism and confirmation, 46; convokes, unites, and sends, 55; fosters dignity, 58; sanctifying and unifying, 70; encourages the rise of lay associations, 102; permeates and transforms peoples 229; activity since Pentecost, 301.

HOPE: 23, 24, 37, 58, 74, 83, 104, 107.

HOUSES OF FORMATION: lack of programs of missionary formation, 127; teaching languages and communications techniques, 285.

HOUSING: decent for the poor, 172, 218.

HUMAN BEING: created good, in God's image, 9, 279; in the new evangelization, 13; revealed by Jesus Christ, 13; free and conscious of dignity, 24; aim of new evangelization is to form, 26; anxieties and hopes; 58; not an abstract being, 157; neither master nor arbiter over his or her own life, 215; urban and rural, 255; in project of education, 265; ready to dominate the world, 266.

HUMAN DEVELOPMENT: goals of new evangelization, 1; in the first evangelization, 19; central idea of the Fourth Conference, 22; based on the resurrection, 24, 33; nourished by holiness, 31; supported by the liturgy, 35; task of the local Church, 55; role of the permanent deacon in, 76; in priestly formation, 84; woman's contribution to, 90; presence of lay people in, 103; in youth pastoral work, 120; actions to defend, 138; relationship to evangelization, 157; duty of all, 157; leads to creating more human living conditions, 162; most pressing demands, 175; in *mestizo*, indigenous, and African American cultures, 251; relationship to culture, 279; Church's commitment, 292, 302.

HUMAN RIGHTS: task of theologians in defending, 33; proclaimed by the Church and guaranteed by Christ, 164, 165; advancing consciousness of, 166; promoting, 168; of indigenous people and African Americans, 251; inviolability of the right to life, 268; to religious formation; 272.

IBERIAN CATHOLICISM: 18.

IDENTITY: of Latin American peoples, 13, 18, 20, 85, 96, 150, 244, 281.

IDEOLOGIES: 26, 62.

IDOLATRY: 154.

IGNORANCE: 39, of religious doctrine, 41, 270.

ILLITERACY: 267.

IMPUNITY: 233.

INCARNATION: of the gospel in today's world, 60; of the Word, 30; and Christian presence in the social and cultural context, 243.

INCULTURATION: of the gospel, 13, 15, 24, 30, 33, 49, 53, 84, 87, 102, 128, 177, 224, 230, 253, 256; of the liturgy, 43, 248; of the faith, 55, 58; of the Church, 248.

INDIFERENTISM: 102; 152; 153; 154, 167.

INDIGENOUS PEOPLE: contribution to work of evangelization, 19; defense and protection of, 20; vocations, 80; condemning abuses against them, 107, 167, 174, 248, 251; promoting the development of women, 109, 110; adolescents and young people, 119; non-Christian religions among, 137; their idea of land, 172; living alongside other ethnic groups, 244; their human and cultural values, 245, 248.

INDIVIDUALISM: 253.

INEQUALITY: social, 24.

INFLATION: 178, 196, 198, 199.

INFORMATION PROCESSING: 280.

INJUSTICE: as breaking solidarity between human beings, 9; denunciation of by prophets, 19, 20; has intensified since Puebla, 23; response of new evangelization, 24; poses challenges to new evangelization, 72; must be combatted, 157; in peoples in which Christian faith has sunk deep roots, 161; condemned in social pastoral work, 200; in market economy, 202.

INSECURITY: 187.

INSENSITIVITY: social, 233.

INTEGRATION: of deacons into diocesan body of priests, 77; of countries, 174; Latin American, 209.

INTERDEPENDENCE: 204, 205.

ISLAM: 138, 147.

JESUS CHRIST: close to the outcast, 4; we enter the reign through, 5; the reign present in him, 5; identified with the mystery of the reign, 5; institutes eucharist, 6; communicates his life to us, 7; guide, hope, and light for human beings, 8; true God and true man, 8; frees us from death, 9; acquired the Church with his blood, 11; offers salvation, 12; invites to plenitude, 13; united to all human beings 13; will bring God's reign to fulfillment, 14; expressed in fraternal love, 23; wealth present in, 24; gives meaning to everything, 27; inexhaustible riches of, 30; Church founds its source in, 31; as evangelizer, 33; prophetic function of, 33; present in the liturgy, 34; good news for our peoples, 37; encountering him leads us to conversion, 46; saving ministry of made present, 66; sources of priestly life flow from, 70; head of the Church, 74; basis for the spirituality of deacons, 77; calls lay believers, 94; fullness of times, 104; restores woman's dignity, 104; goes through the stages of human life, 111; reveals the Father, 121; draws us into the Trinitarian mystery, 121; moral teacher, 154; deeds, 159; perfects equality among human beings, 164; is the standard of everything human, 228; assumes the conditions of peoples, 243; paradigm of every personal attitude, 254; model of communicator, 279; the same yesterday, today, and forever, 287.

JUDAISM: 134, 138.

JUSTICE: aided by theological work, 33; promoted by the spirituality of following Jesus, 116; must be restored, 157; promoting it on the basis of gospel values, 168; relationship to ecology, 169, 171; distributive and the economy, 195; in Latin American integration, 209; in the light of Jesus Christ, 296.

KERYGMA: root of all evangelization, 33; first proclamation, 41; preached in a living and joyful way, 131.

KIDNAPPINGS: 210.

LAND: first sign of God's covenant with humankind, 171; use of, 171; for indigenous people, sacred place, 172; commercial view of, 172; Christian vision of, 173, 176; in Latin America and Caribbean; 174; administration and use of, 175; in theological reflection, 177.

LATIN AMERICA AND THE CARIBBEAN: forces of death in, 9; new ardor for evangelization, 12; evangelization in, 13; Mary, mother of, 15; people chosen by God, 16; arrival of the faith, 16; values, 17; amalgamation (*mestizaje*) in, 18; Church's commitment, 22; delicate and difficult situation, 22, 23, 279; first evangelization, 24; new people in, 32; bishops, 33; baptized people who did not adhere to the gospel, 33; monastic and contemplative life in, 37; challenges to the Church, 38; signs and actions proper to these cultures, 53; communion, 76; religious life, 85; missionary service to evangelize, 91; challenges to religious, 91; ministries conferred on lay people; movements with their own identity, 102; women's presence in the evangelization of, 109; presence of scandalous levels of poverty, 122; presence of fundamentalist sects, 140; efforts to change prevailing policies, 179; consequences of a new international order, 194; association of nations, 205; growing population of children, 221; fidelity to Jesus Christ, 232; multiethnic and multicultural continent, 244; marked by Western culture, 252; urbanization process, 255; proclamation of faith, 302.

LAY LEADERS: in base communities, 61; in communion with the pastor and bishops, 63; missionary leadership, 128, 101.

LAY PEOPLE: integral formation of, 42, 60, 99; their participation in the parish, 59; responsibilities of, 60; task in Christian base communities, 61; commitment to vocational work, 80; co-workers with bishops and priests, 91; make up the majority in the Church, 94; ministries, services, and functions of, 95; pastors neglect of, 96; some have clerical mentality, 96; active agents of the new evangelization, 97, 103, 293, 302;

MEDELLIN: continuity of the Fourth Conference along the same lines, 1, 179, 296.

MEDIA: effects on social groups, 26; not guided by gospel principles, 96; abuses of women in, 107; analyzing messages critically, 108; effect of propaganda and advertising, 112; pastoral approach to, 131; used by sects, 140; life style they spread, 199; contribution to crisis of the family, 216; spread situation morality, 236; manipulative, 238; enormous power of, 253; forming a critical conscience toward, 277; pastoral actions, 280.

MESTIZAJE: 18, 244, 247.

METHODS: observe, judge, act, revise, and celebrate, 119; for approaching the poor, 180; of family planning, 226.

MIGRATION: one of Latin America's ills, 9, 107, 110; its connection to loss of religious roots, 130; Church's activity in this field, 141; seen from the standpoint of faith, 178; Jesus Christ experienced, 186; has increased, 187; no measures to halt, 187; role of government, 188; catechesis for migrants, 189.

MILITARY: to serve democracy and freedom, 99; pastoral work with young people in the military, 119.

MINISTRIES: of reconciliation, 6; diversity of, 23; prophetic, 33, 63, 227; complementarity of, 55; episcopal, 67; priestly, 68, 71; conferred on lay people, 101, 104, 258.

MISSION: of pilgrim Church, 12, of small communities, 48; connected to communion, 55; to the nations, 57; in the parish, 58; woman's, 90; of adolescents and young people, 111.

MISSIONARIES: 21.

MISSIONARY SPIRIT: 56, 63.

MODERNITY: dialogue of with the gospel, 24; positive and negative features, 254; effects on human being, 255.

MORALITY: in fundamentalist sects, 140; undermined by indifference and secularism, 154; utilitarian and individualistic, 169; Christian, 231, 237; of situation, 236.

MURDER: violation of human rights, 167.

MUSIC: in human growth, 119.

NATURE: 233, 252.

NEOLIBERALISM: 181, 199.

NEW CULTURE: created through pastoral activity, 116; urban, 253; of the image, 279.

NEW ECONOMIC ORDER: 194, 296.

NEW EDUCATION: 266.

NEW EVANGELIZATION: driven by the Holy Spirit, 1; in ardor, 1, 12, 28, 33, 288; in expressions, 1, 28, 30, 101, 115; in methods, 1, 28, 29, 101, 297; time of reconciliation, 6; invitation to conversion, 9; firmly established and mature in faith, 12; proclaims the gospel, 13; sheds light on the Fourth Conference, 22; strategy, 22; starting point of, 23, 24; what it is, 24; relationship to first evangelization, 24; content of, 24, 27; subject of, 25; purpose of, 26, 57, 124; addressees, 26, 97; task, 26; what it should be like, 28; inculturated in the world, 30; relationship to holiness, 32; role of the liturgy, 35; demands of, 45; condition for its efficacy, 48; emphasizing *kerygmatic* catechesis, 49; challenges, 59, 154, 230; task of urban parishes, 60; relationship with family pastoral work, 64; agents, 72; 84, 87, 97; commitment of priests, 72; relationship to human development, 76; presence of laity, 103; enhances woman's dignity, 105; commitment to universal mission, 125; relationship to education, 263; call to all, 302.

NEW HEAVEN AND NEW EARTH: 14.

NEW MISSIONARY FERVOR: 124.

NON-CHRISTIANS: 125.

OBEDIENCE: to pope and bishop, 143.

OCCULT: 147, 115.

OLD PEOPLE: abandonment of them, an evil in Latin America, 9; lack of a decent life for, 178; regarded as useless, 219.

ORGANIZATIONS: of peasants and indigenous people, 176, 177; for economic solidarity, 181; of workers, 185; political party, 192.

PEACE: 6, 99, 138.

PEASANTS: pastoral work with youth aimed at, 119; violence against their rights, 167; situation, 172; causes of their living conditions 174; alternatives so that they will not leave their lands, 189.

PEDAGOGY: experiential, participatory, and transforming, 119.

PERMANENT DEACONS: agents of the new evangelization, 25; in communion with priests, 67; permanent formation of, 69; pastoral activity directed at them, 75; their importance in the service of communion in Latin America, 75; service on the continent, 75; recognition of, 77; accompanying in discernment, 77; spirituality of, 77; twofold sacramentality of married, 77; their collaboration in developing the services the Church provides, 77.

PERMISSIVENESS: 154, 235.

PHILOSOPHIES: 147, 253.

PILGRIMAGES TO SHRINES: 53.

PLURALISM: 238.

POLITICIANS: 178.

POLITICS: 96, 99, 179.

POOR: experience solidarity through the witness of religious life, 85; women are sensitive to cry of, 90; evangelization of, 95; teach us how to live in moderation and to share, 169; addressees of the message of Jesus, 178; reveal Jesus' face, 178; serving them fraternally a priority, 180; living conditions worsen as a result of economic adjustment measures, 196.

POPE: successor of Peter, 33; head of college of bishops, 55; adherence of religious to, 85.

POPULAR PIETY: 53.

POPULAR RELIGIOSITY: in the process of racial mixture, 18; expression of inculturation of the faith, 36, 247; its expression multiplied in the Church, 38; presents elements foreign to Catholic religion, 39; need to purify, 53; should be oriented toward conversion, 240.

POPULORUM PROGRESSIO **FOUNDATION:** 251.

PORNOGRAPHY: 235, 280.

POSTMODERNITY: 24, 252.

POVERTY: caused by the lack of consistency between faith and life, 161; a kind of human rights violation, 167; scourge of, 179; witness of Saint Francis, 170.

PRAYER: Church discovers the meaning of its calling in, 34; expresses faith, 37; is part of apostolic mission, 47; of Jesus Christ, 54, 78; liturgical and private, 71; basis of vocational pastoral work, 80; of lay believers, 101; in apostolic movements, 102; translates missionary cooperation of people of God, 128; for Christian unity, 135; in the home, 225.

PREFERENTIAL OPTION FOR THE POOR: basis for, 178; fidelity to, 179; assumed with renewed decision, 180; includes preferential option for the means to enable the poor to rise from their misery, 275; assuming it with new ardor, 296, 302.

PRIESTS: come from the very mystery of God, 70; commitment to new evangelization, 72; old and sick, 73; ongoing training of, 84; should appreciate and accept women, 108.

PRISONERS: 180.

PROFESSIONAL PEOPLE: 204, 283.

PROSELYTISM: of sectarian Christian groups, 133; of fundamentalist sects, 139, 140; of para-Christian or semi-Christian movements, 147; of social and religious enterprises, 147.

PROSTITUTION: 112, 235.

PUBLISHING HOUSES: Catholic, 286.

PUEBLA CONFERENCE: continuity of Fourth Conference with, 1, 196, 247; guidelines with regard to ministries conferred on lay people, 101; proclaimed the preferential option for young people, 114; proposed mission to the nations, 125.

RACISM: 246, 249.

RECONCILIATION: from Jesus, 6, 14; experience of in the Church, 68; part of liberation from sin, 123; should be promoted in the new evangelization, 168.

REIGN OF GOD: entry through faith and following Jesus, 5; present in his life and words, 5; proclaiming him in evangelization, 27, 33; service of ordained ministry, 67; reign of justice, love, and peace in, 204.

RELATIVISM: 154.

RELIGIOUS: agents of evangelization, 19; alongside indigenous, 20; agents of new evangelization, 25; unity with the diocese, 68; heroic witness of, 85; in the work of evangelization, 91; unity with bishops and priests, 93; effective evangelizers 104; serving education, 275.

RELIGIOUS LIFE: 85; renewal of, 85.

RESPECT FOR LIFE: 20.

RIGHTS: demand of the gospel, 13; defended by evangelizers, 20; of the Church, 69; of women, 105; violation of, 167; to the goods of creation, 171; of the worker, 184; of the child, 227; to land, 251; to life, inviolability of the, 268; to religious formation, 272.

RIO DE JANEIRO CONFERENCE: 1, 169.

RITUALISM: 43.

SACRAMENTS: pedagogical value of liturgical celebration of, 35; manifest divine charity, 45; of penance, 46, 151, 225, 232, 240; manifest the Church alive and in operation, 67; communicate and announce the communion of the Church, 123; the newness of Jesus Christ discovered in them, 131.

SAINT MARY OF GUADALUPE: 15, 289.

SAINTS: in the first evangelization, 19; of the Americas, 21; the best evangelizers, 28; in catechesis, 142.

SALVATION: made present in the liturgy, 34; attained by God's grace, 45; eschatological, 157; goal of evangelization, 243.

SCIENCE: contribution to culture, 29; imprint on groups and populations, 26; not guided by gospel criteria, 96.

not see it, 39; develop a gospel sense of, 156; human dignity not lost through, 159; affects relationship with God and with creation, 164.

SINGLE MOTHERS: vulnerable, 110, 218.

SLAVE TRADE: 20.

SLAVES: 20, 246.

SOCIAL SECURITY: 188.

SOCIAL TEACHING OF THE CHURCH: necessary part of preaching, 50; to serve the new evangelization, 76; concept of 158; ideologies incompatible with, 168; communicating and putting into practice, 200; contribution to eduction, 271.

SOLIDARITY: expressed in the eucharist, 6; with those who suffer most, 32; aided by work of theologians, 33; grows in community celebration, 52; among ordained ministries, 75; practice of religious life, 85; in the family, 106; promoted by youth pastoral work, 116, 120; in the gospel message, 157; as service to those in need, 159; necessary value, 159; in the market economy, 195; in combatting drugs, 241; in the emerging culture, 268; in Christian education, 271; in the economic, social, and political order, 296.

SPIRITISM: 147, 155.

SPIRITUAL DIRECTION: lay people need, 42; extends the sacrament or reconciliation, 46; basis for vocational pastoral work, 80; in seminaries, 83; for making a discernment of problems in life, 151.

SPIRITUAL RETREATS: 71.

SPIRITUALITY: renewed, 45; priestly, 70; of permanent deacons, 77; of lay believers, 95, 98, 99; of following Jesus Christ, 116; of the missionary team, 128; to recover the sense of God, 169.

STERILIZATION: 110, 219, 223.

STRUCTURES: at the service of the community, 69; church, 98; unjust economic, 163; and pastoral methods, 180; internal church organization, 209; of sin, 243.

STUDENTS: 119.

SUFFERING: 23, 32.

SYMBOLS: in education, 109; of the liturgy, 248.

SYNCRETISM: religious, 138, 147.

SYNODS OF BISHOPS: of 1990, 70; of 1987, 101.

TEACHERS: why teach and to what end, 265; agent of evangelization, 265; ongoing training of, 273; religious, 275.

TECHNOLOGY: marks social groups, 26; human being should not be subject to, 27; in proclaiming the gospel, 29; in exploiting the earth, 174; changes relationships among human beings, 255.

TELECOMMUNICATIONS: 280.

TERRORISM: an evil in Latin America, 9; violates human rights, 167; expression of the culture of death, 219, 235.

UNBELIEF: 153.

UNDEREMPLOYMENT: 112.

UNEMPLOYED: 183; 199, 218.

UNITY: among ministries and charisms, 23; in diversity, 27, 75; sought by Jesus, 54, 132; springs from the eucharist, 55; not always reflected in the Church, 68; among pastors, 68; in lay councils, 98; in spirits and hearts, 157; of the family 238; of human beings and world in God, 248.

UNIVERSAL CIVILIZATION: new, 255.

UNIVERSALITY OF MESSAGE OF JESUS CHRIST: 7.

UNIVERSITIES: Catholic, 268, 276.

URBANIZATION: 26, 255.

VALUES: of first evangelization, 24; of the reign, 85, 247; of the contemporary world, 87; Christian, within identity of culture, 96; woman's, 107, 108; of the human person, 109; promoting certain fundamental, 169, 200, 204, 252, 274; human and Christian, 214, 233; of culture, 229, 282; disappearing as a result of cultural crisis, 230; new, in agreement with Christian message, 230; rescuing lost, 237; in indigenous peoples, 245; in African American cultures, 246; native cultural, 248; merely subjective social consent, 253; of urban person, 256; in education, 265, 266 (cf. **JESUS CHRIST**).

VATICAN COUNCIL II: new evangelization consistent with, 30; began liturgical renewal, 43; fidelity to, 53; ecclesiology of, 57; renewal of religious starting with, 85; community dimension of the priestly ministry, 68; associations of the apostolate, 102.

VIOLENCE: against women, 106; in sexual relations, 110; against rights of children, women, and poor people, 167; daily and indiscriminate, 178; causes terror, 179; growing in Latin America, 235.

VIRGINITY: 89.

VOCATION: of every human being, 13, 159; conditions to mature in, 42; variety and complementarity of, 55; increasing, 79, 82; commitment of lay people to promote, 80; from all cultures, 80; to contemplative life, 86; of baptized, 94; discovery and maturing of, 96; woman's, 96, 108; in pastoral work with young people, 114; human being's co-creative, 182.

VOLUNTARY REPATRIATION: 187.

WAR: 2, 219.

WISDOM: to find new methods and new expressions, 1; of our peoples, 36, 169.

WITNESS: of the unity of the Church, 23; forms part of new methods for new evangelization, 29; of the whole people of God, 33, 128, 156; expression of Christian worship, 34; in priestly life, 71, 145; of permanent deacons, 75; of religious men and women, 85; in contemplative life, 86; in pastoral activity, 200.

WOMEN: utilization of, 9; agent of new evangelization, 25; in religious life, 90; equality with men, 104; nature and mission, 105; guardian angel of Christian soul of the continent, 106; abuses against, 107; acceptance of and appreciation for, 108; discriminated against in education, 109; assaults on dignity of, 110; humiliated and disregarded, 178.

WORD OF GOD: brings together faithful and pastors, 11; transmitted to human beings through action of the Holy Spirit, 31; nourishes catechesis, 33, 294; in the work of theologians, 33; casts light on the situation of peoples, 49; in pilgrimages and religious celebrations, 53; aimed at lay

Appendix I

JOHN PAUL II'S MESSAGE
TO INDIGENOUS PEOPLE

Beloved Indigenous Brothers and Sisters of the American Continent,

1.   In commemorating the Fifth Centenary of the Beginning of the Evangelization of the New World, there is a special place in the Pope's heart and affection for the descendants of the men and women who populated this Continent when the cross of Christ was planted there on October 12, 1492.

From the Dominican Republic, where I had the joy of meeting some of your representatives, I send my message of peace and love to all the indigenous ethnic groups and their members, from the Alaskan peninsula to Tierra del Fuego. You are the heirs of the peoples—TupiGuaraní Aymara, Maya Quechua Chibcha Nahualt, Mixtecó, Araucano Yanomani, Guajiro, Inuit, Apaches, and so many others—who were known for their nobility of spirit, whose autochthonous cultural values stood out, such as the Aztec, Inca, and Mayan civilizations, and who can be proud of the fact that they have a view of life that recognizes the sacredness of the world and of the human person. Simplicity, humility, love of freedom, hospitality, solidarity, attachment to the family, a closeness to the earth, and a sense of contemplation are some of the many values that America's indigenous memory has kept to this very day and which are a contribution that can be found in the Latin American soul.

2.   Five hundred years ago the Gospel of Jesus Christ came to your peoples. Even before that, however, even though no one suspected it, the living and true God was present, enlightening your paths. The Apostle John tells us that the Word, the Son of God, is "the true Light which enlightens everyone who comes into this world" (Jn 1:9). Indeed, the "seeds of the Word" were already present and enlightening the hearts of your ancestors that they might discover the imprint of God the Creator in all his creatures: sun, moon, mother earth, volcanoes and forests, lakes and rivers.

However, in the light of the Good News, they discovered that all the wonders of creation were but a pale reflection of their Author and that the

-184-

human person, because he is the image and likeness of the Creator, is much higher than the material world and is called to an eternal, transcendent destiny. Jesus of Nazareth, the Son of God made man, freed us from sin by his death and resurrection, making us God's adoptive children and opening up for us the path to life without end. The message of Jesus Christ made them see that all people are brothers and sisters because they have a common Father: God. And all are called to form part of the one Church which the Lord founded with his blood (cf. Acts 20:28).

In the light of Christian revelation, the ancient values of your ancestors, such as hospitality, solidarity, a spirit of generosity, reached their fullness in the great commandment of love, which must be the Christian's supreme law. The conviction that evil is identified with death and good with life opened up to them the heart of Jesus, who is "the Way, the Truth, and the Life" (Jn 14:6).

All of this, which the Fathers of the Church call the "seeds of the Word," were purified, deepened, and completed by the Christian message which proclaims universal brotherhood and defends justice. Jesus said that those who thirst for justice are blessed (cf. Mt 5:6). What motive other than preaching the gospel ideals impelled so many missionaries to denounce the abuses committed against the *Indios* with the arrival of the *conquistadors*? To demonstrate this, we have the apostolic activity and the writings of intrepid Spanish evangelists like Bartolomé de Las Casas, Fray Antonio de Montesinos, Vasco de Quiroga, Juan del Valle, Julián Garcés, José de Anchieta Manuel de Nóbrega, and so many other men and women who generously devoted their lives to the natives. The Church has always been at the side of the indigenous people through her religious priests and bishops; in this Fifth Centenary, how could she possibly forget the enormous suffering inflicted on the peoples of this Continent during the age of conquest and colonization! In all truth, there must be a recognition of the abuses committed due to a lack of love on the part of some individuals who did not see their indigenous brothers and sisters as children of God their Father.

3.   In this commemoration of the Fifth Centenary, I want to repeat what I said during my first pastoral visit to Latin America: "The Pope and the Church are with you and love you; they love your persons, your culture, your traditions; they admire your marvelous past, they encourage you in the present, and hope so much for the future" (*Address at Cuilapan,* January 29, 1979 [English trans., see *L'Osservatore Romano,* February 12, 1979]). Therefore, I want to become the echo and spokesman of your deepest longing.

I know you want to be respected as persons and citizens. The Church, on her part, makes her own your legitimate aspiration, since your dignity is no less than that of any other person or race. Every man and woman has been created in the image and likeness of God (cf. Gn 1:26-27). Jesus, who always showed his preference for the poor and abandoned, tells us that whatever we do or fail to do "for one of these least brothers of mine," we do for him (cf. Mt 25:40). No one who claims to be a Christian can reject or discriminate against anyone because of race or culture. The Apostle Paul admonishes us to have respect: "For in one Spirit we were all baptized into one body, whether Jews or Greeks, slaves or free persons" (1 Cor 12:13).

Faith, dear brothers and sisters, overcomes the differences between people. The faith and baptism give life to a new people: the people of the children of God. Without a doubt, although it overcomes differences, faith does not destroy them but respects them. The unity of all of us in Christ does not signify, from the human point-of-view, uniformity. On the contrary, the ecclesial communities feel enriched by welcoming the manifold diversity and variety of all their members.

4.   Therefore, the Church encourages indigenous peoples to maintain and promote with legitimate pride the culture of their peoples: their healthy traditions and customs, their own language and values. In defending your identity, you are not only exercising your right; you are also fulfilling your duty to hand on your culture to future generations, thus enriching the whole of society. This cultural dimension, with its effects on evangelization, will be one of the priorities of the Fourth General Conference of the Latin American Episcopate, which I had the joy of inaugurating as the most important act of this visit on the occasion of the Fifth Centenary.

Protection of and respect for cultures, making good use of all that is positive in them, doubtlessly does not mean that the Church is renouncing her mission of elevating customs, rejecting everything that is in opposition to or contradicts gospel morality. "The Church's mission," the *Puebla Conclusions* states, "is to bear witness to 'the true God and one Lord.' So there is nothing insulting in the fact that evangelization invites peoples to abandon false conceptions of God, unnatural patterns of conduct, and aberrant manipulations of some people by others" (405-406).

A central element of indigenous cultures is their attachment and nearness to mother earth. You love the land and want to keep in contact with nature. I join my voice to that of those who are asking for the adoption of strategies and means to protect and preserve nature, which God has created. Due respect for the environment must always be held above purely economic interests or the abusive exploitation of the resources of land and sea.

5. Among the problems that afflict many indigenous communities are those related to land ownership. I know that the Church's pastors, based on the demands of the gospel and in harmony with her social magisterium, have consistently supported your legitimate rights, promoting proper agrarian reform and urging everyone to solidarity as the sure path to justice. I also know the difficulty you have in regard to topics such as social security, the right of association, the empowerment of farmers, participation in the national life, the integral formation of your children, education, health care, housing, and so many other problems that concern you. In this regard, I am reminded of the words that I addressed several years ago to the *Indios* during that memorable meeting in Quetzaltenango: "The Church knows, beloved sons and daughters, the social discrimination that you suffer, the injustices that you bear, the serious difficulties you have in defending your lands and your rights, the frequent lack of respect for your customs and traditions. For this reason, in carrying out her task of evangelization, the Church wants to stay close to you and to raise her voice of condemnation when your dignity as human beings and children of God is violated; she wishes to accompany you peacefully, as the gospel demands, but with resolve and energy, in achieving the recognition and the promotion of your dignity and your rights as persons" (*Address at Quetzaltenango,* March 7, 1983 [English trans., see *L'Osservatore Romano,* May 9, 1983]).

Within the context of the religious mission that is hers, the Church will spare no effort in continuing to encourage all those initiatives aimed at promoting the common good and integral development of your communities, in addition to fostering legislation that respects and adequately protects the authentic values and rights of the indigenous peoples. A proof of this determined desire for cooperation and assistance can be seen in the Holy See's recent establishment of the *Populorum Progressio* Foundation, which has a fund to help the poorest indigenous groups and rural populations of Latin America.

I encourage you, then, to make a renewed commitment to be actively involved in your own spiritual and human growth through dignified and constant labor, fidelity to the best of your traditions, and the practice of virtue. For this, you can count on the genuine values of your culture, refined over time by the generations who have preceded you in this blessed land. Most of all, however, you can count on the greatest wealth which you have received by God's grace, your Catholic faith. Following the teaching of the gospel, you will succeed in making your people, faithful to their legitimate traditions, progress materially as well as spiritually. Enlightened by faith in

Jesus Christ, you will recognize other people as your brothers and sisters over and above any difference in race or culture. Faith will enlarge your hearts so that you can accept all your fellow citizens. This same faith will lead others to love you, to respect your characteristics, and to join with you in building a future in which everyone will take an active and responsible part, as is fitting to Christian dignity.

6. Concerning your proper place in the Church, I urge everyone to promote those pastoral initiatives that foster the indigenous communities' greater integration and participation. For this, renewed effort will have to be made in whatever is related to the inculturation of the gospel since "a faith which does not become culture is a faith which has not been fully received nor thoroughly thought through nor faithfully lived out" (*Address to the World of Culture,* Lima, May 15, 1988 [English trans., see *L'Osservatore Romano,* June 20, 1988]). Ultimately, it is a question of indigenous Catholics becoming the agents of their own development and evangelization in all areas, including the various ministries. What a great joy it will be to see the day when your communities can be served by missionaries, priests, and bishops who have come from your own families and can guide you in adoring God "in spirit and truth" (Jn 4:23)!

The message that I entrust to you in the American land today, commemorating five centuries of the gospel's presence among you, is intended to be a call to hope. The Church, which has been with you in your journey throughout these 500 years, will do everything in her power to help the descendants of the ancient peoples of America to occupy their rightful place in society and the ecclesial communities. I am aware of the serious problems and difficulties you face. However, be sure that you will never lack God's help and the protection of his most holy Mother, as was promised once on Tepeyac hill to the *Indio* Juan Diego, an illustrious son of your own blood, whom I had the joy of raising to the honors of the altar: "Listen and understand, my littlest son, that nothing should frighten or bother you; do not let your heart be troubled, do not fear this infirmity, nor any other infirmity or anxiety. Am I not here, your mother? Are you not in my shadow? Am I not your protection? Are you not perhaps in my lap?" (*Nican Mopohua*).

May Our Lady of Guadalupe protect all of you. I cordially bless you in the name of the Father, and of the Son, and of the Holy Spirit. Amen.

Given at Santo Domingo, October 12, 1992, the Fifth Centenary of the Evangelization of America.

Appendix II

JOHN PAUL II'S MESSAGE TO AFRICAN AMERICANS

Dearly Beloved African American Brothers and Sisters,

1. The Fifth Centenary of the Evangelization of the New World is an appropriate occasion to address my message of encouragement to you from the city of Santo Domingo. May it increase your hope and sustain your Christian commitment, renewing the vitality of your communities to which, as Successor of Peter, I send an intimate and affectionate greeting in the words of the Apostle Paul: "We wish you the favor and peace of God our Father, and of the Lord Jesus Christ" (Gal 1:3).

The evangelization of America is a reason for giving heartfelt thanks to God who, in his infinite mercy, wanted the message of salvation to reach the inhabitants of this blessed land, made fruitful by the cross of Christ, which has left an imprint on the life and history of his people and has produced such abundant fruits of holiness and virtue throughout the span of these five centuries.

The date of October 12, 1492 marks the initial encounter of races and cultures that feature in the history of these 500 years, during which the penetrating Christian gaze enables us to discover God's loving intervention, in spite of human shortcomings and faithlessness. In fact, in the course of history, there is a mysterious confluence of sin and grace, but in the long run, grace triumphs over the power of sin. As Saint Paul tells us: "Despite the increase of sin, grace has far surpassed it" (Rom 5:20).

2. In these celebrations of the Fifth Centenary, I could not fail to bring my message of closeness and warm affection to the African American peoples who are an important part of the population of the whole Continent; they enrich the Church and society in so many countries with their human and Christian values, as well as with their culture. In this context, the words of Simón Bolivar come to mind. He declared that "America is the result of the union of Europe and Africa with aborigine elements. That is why there is no room there for racial prejudice, and if it were to appear, America would return to a state of primitive chaos."

Everyone is aware of the serious injustice committed against those black peoples of the African continent who were violently torn from their land, their culture, and their traditions, and shipped to America as slaves. During my recent apostolic visit to Senegal, I did not want to omit a visit the Island of Gorée, where this ignominious trade began; I wanted to show the Church's firm repudiation of it with words that I should now like to recall: "The visit to the 'slave house' recalls to mind that enslavement of black people which in 1462 Pius II, writing to a missionary bishop who was leaving for Guinea, described as an 'enormous crime,' the *magnum scelus*.' Throughout a whole period of the history of the African continent, black men and women and children were brought to this cramped space, uprooted from their land and separated from their loved ones to be sold as goods. They came from all different countries and, parting in chains for new lands, they retained as the last image of their native Africa Gorée's basalt rock cliffs. We could say that this island is fixed in the memory and heart of all the black diaspora. These men, women and children were the victims of a disgraceful trade in which people who were baptized, but who did not live their faith, took part. How can we forget the enormous suffering inflicted, the violation of the most basic human rights, on those people deported from the African Continent? How can we forget the human lives destroyed by slavery? In all truth and humility this sin of man against man, this sin of man against God, must be confessed" (*Speech on the Island of Gorée,* February 22, 1992).

3.   Looking at the current situation in the New World, we see vigorous and thriving African American communities which, without forgetting their past history, contribute the wealth of their cultures to the wide variety of culture on the Continent. With a tenacity not free from sacrifice they contribute to the common good, becoming integrated in the social whole but preserving their own identity, traditions, and customs. This fidelity to their own being and spiritual heritage is something that the Church not only respects but encourages and desires to strengthen; since human beings—all human beings—are created in the image and likeness of God (cf. Gn 1:26-27), any genuinely human reality is an expression of this image, regenerated by Christ through his redemptive sacrifice.

By means of Christ's redemption, dear African American brothers and sisters, all humanity has passed from the shadow to light, from being "not my people" to being "children of the living God" (Hos 2:1). As "God's chosen ones" we form one body, that is, the Church (cf. Col 3:12-15), in which, in the words of Saint Paul, "there is no Greek or Jew here, circumcised or uncircumcised, foreigner, Scythian, slave or freeman. Rather, Christ is everything in all of you" (Col 3:11). Indeed, faith overcomes the differences between people and gives life to a new people, the people of the children of God. Without exception, while overcoming the differences in the common condition of Christians, faith does not destroy them but respects and dignifies them.

This is why, in commemorating this Fifth Centenary, I urge you to defend your identity, to be conscious of your values and to make them bear fruit. However, as pastor of the Church, I urge you above all to be aware of the great treasure that you have received through God's grace, your Catholic faith. In the light of Christ, you will manage to help your communities to grow and progress spiritually as well as materially, thus spreading the gifts that God has granted you. Illuminated by Christian faith, you will look upon other human beings, regardless of any difference of race or culture, as your brothers and sisters, children of the same Father.

4. The Church's solicitude for you and your communities in view of the new evangelization, human development, and Christian culture will be highlighted at the Fourth General Conference of the Latin American Episcopate, which I had the pleasure of inaugurating yesterday. Without forgetting that many gospel values have penetrated and enriched the culture, mentality, and life of African Americans, there is a desire to increase pastoral attention and to encourage the specific elements of the ecclesial communities in their own expression.

Evangelization does not destroy your values but is incarnated in them; it consolidates and strengthens them. It causes the growth of the seeds scattered by the "Word of God who was in the world as 'the true light that enlightens every man' (Jn 1:9), before becoming flesh to save and gather up all things in himself" (*Gaudium et Spes,* 57). Faithful to the universality of her mission, the Church proclaims Jesus Christ and invites people of all races and conditions to accept his message. As the Latin American Bishops declared at the General Conference of Puebla de los Angeles, "the Church's mission is to bear witness to 'the true God and the one Lord.' So evangelization invites people to abandon false conceptions of God, unnatural patterns of conduct, and aberrant manipulations of some people by others" and cannot be seen as a mere accident (406). Indeed, with evangelization, "the Good News of Christ continually renews the life and culture of fallen man; it combats and removes the error and evil that flow from the ever-present attraction of sin, it never ceases to purify and elevate the morality of peoples. It takes the spiritual qualities and endowments of every age and nation, and with supernatural riches it causes them to blossom, as it were, from within; it fortifies, completes, and restores them in Christ" (*Gaudium et Spes,* 58).

5.   However, the life of many African Americans in various countries is not without hardships and difficulty. Well aware of this, the Church shares your suffering and accompanies you and supports your legitimate aspirations for a more just and dignified life for everyone. In this regard, I cannot refrain from expressing my heartfelt gratitude and from encouraging the apostolic activities of so many priests and religious who are excising their ministry with the poorest and the most destitute. I ask God that your Christian communities may give rise to many vocations to the priesthood and the religious life so that the African Americans of the Continent may be able to rely on ministers from their own families.

While I entrust you to the motherly protection of the blessed Virgin to whom devotion is so widespread in the life and Christian practices of African American Catholics, I bless you in the name of the Father, and of the Son, and of the Holy Spirit. Amen.

Given at Santo Domingo, October 12, 1992, the Fifth Centenary of the Evangelization of America.